Abraham Lincoln
and
The Union

by Oscar Handlin

BOSTON'S IMMIGRANTS: A STUDY IN ACCULTURATION   (1941)

THIS WAS AMERICA   (1949)

THE UPROOTED   (1951)   SECOND EDITION ENLARGED   (1973)

ADVENTURE IN FREEDOM   (1954)

HARVARD GUIDE TO AMERICAN HISTORY   (1954)

AMERICAN PEOPLE IN THE TWENTIETH CENTURY   (1954)

CHANCE OR DESTINY   (1955)

RACE AND NATIONALITY IN AMERICAN LIFE   (1957)

READINGS IN AMERICAN HISTORY   (1957)

AL SMITH AND HIS AMERICA   (1958)

IMMIGRATION AS A FACTOR IN AMERICAN HISTORY   (1959)

JOHN DEWEY'S CHALLENGE TO AMERICAN EDUCATION   (1959)

THE NEWCOMERS: NEGROES AND PUERTO RICANS
IN A CHANGING METROPOLIS   (1959)

AMERICAN PRINCIPLES AND ISSUES: THE NATIONAL PURPOSE   (1961)

THE AMERICANS   (1963)

FIRE-BELL IN THE NIGHT: THE CRISIS IN CIVIL RIGHTS   (1964)

CHILDREN OF THE UPROOTED   (1966)

STATUE OF LIBERTY   (1971)

PICTORIAL HISTORY OF IMMIGRATION   (1972)

TRUTH IN HISTORY   (1979)

with Mary F. Handlin

COMMONWEALTH: A STUDY OF THE ROLE OF GOVERNMENT
IN AMERICAN ECONOMY   (1947)

DIMENSIONS OF LIBERTY   (1961)

POPULAR SOURCES OF POLITICAL AUTHORITY   (1966)

THE AMERICAN COLLEGE AND AMERICAN CULTURE   (1970)

FACING LIFE: YOUTH AND THE FAMILY IN AMERICAN HISTORY   (1971)

THE WEALTH OF THE AMERICAN PEOPLE   (1975)

with Lilian Handlin

ABRAHAM LINCOLN AND THE UNION   (1980)

Oscar and Lilian Handlin

Abraham Lincoln
and
The Union

 HarperCollins*Publishers*

ISBN 0-673-39340-2
9101112131415-HPI-969594939291

Frontispiece courtesy of The Bettman Archive

for Edith Bombach

Preface

YET ANOTHER Lincoln biography?

Surely few subjects have received as extensive treatment as Abraham Lincoln. Competent books cover the whole of his life and every aspect of it — his family, his friends, his reading, thinking, and writing. Perhaps Napoleon alone among historical characters has attracted as much attention.

But yes, there is something more to say.

The endless fascination of this man derives from a combination of qualities in counterpoise — strength and frailty, faith and skepticism, rationality and emotion. The interplay among these attributes, from boyhood to maturity and then to premature old age developed a personality whose common humanity remains rich in interest more than a century after his death.

Then too, this life intersected the critical events of its times and of the history of the United States. Born on the backwoods frontier, Lincoln died as his country advanced into the high stages of industrialization. The experience of secession and civil war compelled him to probe the meaning of the Union he had cherished from early youth. And the problem of slavery drew this southerner by birth on to consider the implications of a national dedication to liberty and equality, not only for blacks but also for whites, and not only for Americans but for the whole world.

It was Lincoln's great gift to put into words the thoughts his countrymen recognized, even those they could not themselves articulate. That service he can still render the people of the twentieth century's closing decades.

Our research has uncovered no facts hitherto unknown, but it has encompassed all the facts known. And it has provided us with the means of understanding Abraham Lincoln, his times, and the meaning of both.

Oscar and Lilian Handlin

Contents

Abraham Lincoln
and
The Union

I
Adrift

AT THE POINT of confluence the clearer waters of the Ohio poured across the darker, muddy Mississippi. Now the scenery changed. Ever since the departure from Gentry's Landing in April 1828, the tall trees along the steep banks, the occasional clearings, and sometimes a town offered familiar views to the men on the flatboat. Once they had made the turn and entered the greater swifter river, the swampy shores flattened away; clumps of cottonwood and scrubby brush scarcely broke the distant vistas. Now and then a squatter's cabin, piled about with firewood ready for the passing steamboat, gave a sign of human habitation, different however from the open spaces at home. Few settlements relieved the oppressive loneliness of the landscape, for whoever could retreated well out of sight to escape the ravages of yearly floods. The very course of the waters altered character, no longer pouring directly west, but swirling southward in lazy curves and bends, as they approached strange new lands where trees covered with Spanish moss darkened the forest, in keeping with the deadly malignity of the climate.

The travelers sensed the strangeness in the big places on the way; Natchez and Baton Rouge were cities larger than any they had seen before. They caught unfamiliar views of sugar plantations and then came by the levees, looked down at the homes and lanes below, and glimpsed the many-masted harbor before they tied up with other craft like their own in New Orleans.

The young men had taken on a job, not in the least unusual in their day. The merchant had assembled a cargo of country produce and advanced the funds to build the craft that they were to guide to the New Orleans market. There they could sell both the produce and the timber. The three months spent in the process earned them a tidy sum; and for ten dollars or less they could return upstream by steamboat.

By its population alone, the metropolis of 44,000 astonished beholders who had spent their lives in communities that numbered scarcely a hundred souls. French-speaking passersby, numerous blacks, narrow streets, iron balconies, and picturesque high-roofed houses conveyed a sense of the foreign, as did the ships destined for New York, Havana, Hamburg, Bremen, Vera Cruz, and other such faraway, exotic places. If the undrained swamps and swarming mosquitoes reminded the youth of home, nothing back in Indiana matched the Egyptian mummy on exhibit in a sarcophagus attended by an American dwarf, or the greedy traders, or the bold prostitutes, or the public slave markets.

The experience gave Abraham Lincoln much to think about as he returned up river on the steamboat. He had believed that he knew what lay ahead when he got the chance to go. He had often watched the cargoes of corn, pork, oats, and beans float out of sight on flatboats making the 1200-mile voyage to New Orleans. Indeed, he recalled the stories his father told of such a journey back in 1806 — only then the way back had been a grueling overland trip on foot. When James Gentry, a successful trader in Rockport, Indiana, asked him to go, Abe agreed. He did not consider the job extraordinary; and he had nothing better to do. And the three months down, though interesting and marked by occasional encounters with tricky currents and hazardous passages by rocks and snags, was much as expected. By drifting down river as he had drifted through life he had arrived at the city, which exposed to his bewildered gaze how much of the world lay beyond the narrow boundaries of the home to which he now returned.

Ever restless, the Lincolns had shifted from place to place, never striking permanent roots; a few years' work on one site, somehow, only sharpened the discontent that carried them on to another. Each move was evidence of past failure, future hope; expectations always outran actuality, so that each present day fell short both of yesterday's desires and of wishes for the morrow.

So Thomas Lincoln passed his life, neither the slovenly good-for-nothing failure nor the self-made successful entrepreneur, but somewhere between, verging now in one direction, now in another. He loved a good story, enjoyed rough fellowship and hunting, worked hard, speculated in land, possessed little education and only slightly more religion. While a youth, he had mostly labored as a hired hand on other people's farms and had learned a carpenter's trade. He grew up honest and conscientious but also restless and acquisitive, ever hopeful that yet another journey across the county or state line would bring him and his family closer to realizing some unarticulated dream.

In 1806, while he lived in Elizabethtown, Kentucky, he met and married Nancy Hanks, a neighborhood girl. The high point of the wedding, on June 12, was the traditional Kentucky "infare" — with bear meat, venison, wild turkey, maple sugar lumps tied on a string to bite off for coffee, and the equally customary race for the whiskey barrel.

The twelve years of their marriage exposed the differences in character of husband and wife. Whereas the outgoing Tom relished company and thrived on hard work and opportunity, Nancy — withdrawn, somber, self-sacrificing, and deeply religious — stayed home, begat three children, and endured unending hardship and pain. She wearily followed where her husband led and patiently set up households, only to abandon them soon after. Her features soon lost their youthful freshness and assumed a habitually woeful expression. Nancy could neither read nor write but sometimes showed signs of refinement incongruous with the rough life about her.

The first Lincoln home was a cabin close to the courthouse. A daughter, Sarah, was the prompt fruit of the union. Thomas worked as a carpenter and for $8.92 acquired a dish, some plates, spoons, a basin, and a sword. In 1808 the family moved twice, once to a cabin outside town where Thomas helped on the farm, and then to a place of their own, on the Big South Fork of the Nolin creek, near Hodgenville. Tom paid $200 in cash for 300 acres of land and from the timber in the surrounding woods raised a cabin that boasted one door, one window, a chimney, and a dirt floor. A second child, named Abraham after his grandfather, was born on February 12, 1809.

Lincoln later described those years, borrowing from Gray's *Elegy*, as "the short and simple annals of the poor." The land was inhospitable and difficult to clear. In the small cabin the stifling summers and the cold, wet winters kept the family in constant discomfort.

The boy suffered no illusions about farm life. Knowing its hardships firsthand, he never endowed it with purifying or ennobling attributes. This land dripped with neither milk nor honey, nor did it encourage husbandmen to take ease. It yielded a crop only at the cost of many a blister and with much back-breaking labor. Whoever failed to store provisions for the winter suffered when the snow fell. Scarcity or plenty depended on the graces of the weather. An unexpected storm could wash away a month's work and a parching hot spell destroy a year's harvest. For years Abraham carried about a memory: He followed along, scattering pumpkin seeds between the hills of corn as his father hoed down in the creek bottom. Suddenly the rain fell and a flash flood washed away the seeds, obliterating all signs of the human toil just expended.

At the age of seven Abraham attended his first school at Knob Creek — no windows, one door. There Zachariah Riley and Caleb Hazel heard the pupils bawl the lessons out and taught some reading, writing, and a bit of spelling. Bodily, not intellectual, strength was the teachers' main qualification. Hazel could easily thrash anyone within reach. Abraham learned chiefly that learning would be on his own. He summed up his judgment later: the classroom held absolutely nothing to excite ambition for education.

In December of 1816, Thomas gave up on Kentucky. He judged the land too difficult to clear, and in any case his title was in dispute. The more he considered it, the clearer was the conclusion: in Indiana, across the river, land went for two dollars an acre, and the rich black soil surely assured the family a better life. He traded the old farm for barrels of saleable whiskey, built a flatboat, and set forth down the creek to Salt River, then into the Ohio. He made the new purchase in the Little Pigeon Creek community just taking form in Perry County, Indiana, a place of unbroken woods, then went back the hundred miles on foot to fetch Nancy and the two children. Two horses sufficed to carry all the Lincoln possessions to the new home. Abe moved along with the others, through the thick forests with only a few settlers' huts among the trees, then to the great Ohio River, so different from Knob Creek in its width, shining away as far as the eye could see.

The Lincolns remained in the new home for fourteen years. Northwest of their homestead lay Vincennes, where William H. Harrison had served for twelve years as territorial governor. But now in 1816 Indiana, having framed a constitution, had joined the Union as a state, with Jonathan Jennings its first chief executive. Most of its 64,000 residents, like Thomas, battled the woods to scrape a living from farms. Like him, many were of Southern yeoman stock and, like him at the age of thirty-eight, prepared to start a new life. The economy rested on barter; few had money to spare for costly imported manufactures. Homespun clothing, bare feet in the summer, and shoepacks in the winter were the rule. Game and pork were the chief items of diet, whiskey and water the drinks. Everyone made soap with lye from wood ashes, and only the better off boasted household utensils.

The forests still stood intact when the little family, with borrowed oxen and a sled, made its way through the dense underbrush, chopping away at small trees and bushes, moving aside to pass by fallen oaks across whose immense trunks the moss had overspread. The Lincolns spent their first Indiana winter in a makeshift cabin — open on one side, fourteen feet wide, the earth strewn with leaves, beds made of brush covered with skins. A fire burned continuously at the open end, to scare off marauding animals as well as to provide warmth. When the wind blew one way, smoke filled the little space; when it changed direction, the heat escaped.

In the spring Thomas cleared several acres; he girdled the largest trees and left them to die but felled and burned the smaller ones. After removing the charred remnants he planted corn and pumpkin seeds between the stumps. Meanwhile he also built a new cabin, the largest Abraham remembered, with one bearskin-draped door and no window. Company soon arrived. Nancy's aunt and uncle with their adopted son Dennis settled in, so that seven people shared the tiny space, subsisting on wild turkey and rabbit, illuminating their cabin with bear's grease. The second winter was almost as harsh as the first.

That winter of 1817 was Nancy's last. In October 1818, after having nursed her aunt and uncle, who died, she too came down with the dreaded milk sickness, an epidemic no one could explain. No doctor was within reach. But even had one been available, there was no cure. Nancy's tongue turned white, and seven days of racking pain ended in death. Thomas built a coffin for which little Abraham whittled the pegs that held the planks together. They buried Nancy in a small clearing not far from the cabin.

While little Sarah cared for her brother and for Dennis Hanks, Thomas set off for Elizabethtown in search of a new wife, hopeful that the woman he had tried to marry once before would have him now. Sarah Bush Johnston, a widow with three children, accepted Thomas's proposal. After paying her debts he loaded her furniture and household goods onto a wagon for a winter journey back to Indiana.

Sarah took over the cheerless household and in a short time transformed the crude dull cabin into a home where all children were equally loved, where a window was carved out, and where life became more civilized. Abraham never forgot her kindness, love, and attention — all the qualities of a good and kind mother. Sarah also brought unheard-of luxuries into the woods — polished furniture, a real table with chairs, feather pillows, and some eating utensils. Eight people now shared the cabin.

Death was much on the mind of the nine-year-old boy who watched his mother's coffin lowered into the grave. Nancy's body had waited in the cabin her husband and children used, while they built the coffin and dug a grave in the nearby clearing. Only a little while before, in the same home, Abraham's aunt and uncle had succumbed; and back in Kentucky his younger brother had also lost his life.

Thoughts of death continued to preoccupy the boy, who well knew the sense of helplessness in the little Indiana community when untimely accident or illness struck. A horse's kick in 1819 proved almost fatal. But then everyone recalled the children's prayer, early learned and oft repeated: "If I should die before I wake, I pray the Lord my soul to take." The tales of Indian savagery Thomas spun reminded his son that death lurked in the forests. The stories of patrols that guarded the Kentucky borders against marauders always ended in slaughter and bloodshed. Abraham did not doubt the truth of these accounts; his own grandfather had been a victim of the red men, and his granduncle, at fourteen, had killed a warrior in the intermittent warfare of settlers and tribesmen. Old Indian ghosts still haunted the woods around the Lincoln farm.

No one survived in this environment without knowing the

touch and taste of blood. The everyday hunt for game was a death-dealing act. Frequent attacks by bears and wolves decimated the livestock. When the wolves howled and panthers' screams pierced the night, Abraham and his sister remembered another tale, commonly known in the neighborhood, of two children mauled to death by wild beasts not long before the Lincolns' arrival.

To the questions life's fragility raised the boy found no easy answers. Frequent moves from one isolated residence to another had worn away the habit of church attendance and had deprived the Lincolns of the fund of consolatory wisdom others heard in the familiar sermon phrases or in the clergymen's soothing ministrations. A year passed before a preacher appeared to say a few comforting words over Nancy's crude grave, unmarked but easily seen from the cabin door.

The Lincolns nevertheless would indignantly have rejected any suggestion of atheism. They considered themselves good Christians. Thomas and Nancy, though married by a Methodist circuit rider who happened by, were members of the Little Mount Separate Baptist Church, formed after a dispute over slavery; Thomas, though Southern, utterly opposed any human bondage. The congregation the Lincolns joined also differed from the Regular Kentucky Baptists in rejecting all creedal doctrines except those emanating directly from the Scriptures. Abandoning the Philadelphia Confession of Faith, which tried to regularize churches and uphold an educated ministry, Thomas and Nancy chose a looser form of worship, less demanding on the parishioners and more dependent on the heart than on the book. Formality was rare and became even more so when the family moved to Indiana; months often passed before an itinerant preacher appeared to conduct a service. Yet the Lincolns maintained their faith and remained loyal to their understanding of the Bible. When some twenty families had settled in the Indiana forest about them, they helped raise a small church. Thomas, one of the few skilled carpenters in the vicinity, supervised construction of the meeting house and became one of the founders of the Little Pigeon Creek Baptist Church and a leading member of the congregation. As trustee and moderator he shared responsibility for religious discipline.

The faith was simple and harsh. Providence ruled human affairs and predetermined their minutest details. Neither Nancy nor Thomas ever questioned the righteousness of God's ways but accepted whatever came as part of a course of events to which they could only submit. Struggle as he might, man, sinful and proud, had to come to terms with his nothingness; those destined to salvation would find glorious rest in heaven, those destined to hell would suffer everlasting torment. Still, recognition of their feebleness did not absolve people from the obligation to struggle; on the contrary, it required them to redouble their efforts. Knowledge that storm or drought, in God's will, could wipe away the work of weeks was no excuse for passivity but rather a stimulus to do the work of months, not simply out of prudence but also in the hope of a reward by grace.

These articles of faith encouraged a boy to drift into youth with no clear goal in view. Strenuous effort was an expected part of life — to what purpose was unclear. Nor did this understanding of the world persuade the youngster of the utility of long-term ambitious plans that might remove him from the narrow circle of kin and place.

What light broke through emanated from the printed page. Abraham differed from his contemporaries, not in what books came to hand but in his liking for reading, a skill he acquired through his own efforts.

The Bible was one of the first books in children's hands, in some cabins the only one available. Parents read it aloud in the absence of formal religious services. Abraham early took as a text the Lincoln family Bible, with commentaries by the Reverend Ostervald, Swiss professor of divinity. He memorized and recited passages and learned to apply the proverbs to daily life. The flowing scriptural phrases polished the boy's rough-

hewn everyday language, enriching its texture, expanding its
vocabulary, and instilling ways of thought and modes of reasoning broader and more refined than those evoked by solitary
forest life. Nancy Hanks, though illiterate, told her children
many biblical tales, evoking scenes of a faraway world in which
the righteous got their just rewards. Years later Lincoln recalled the one bright spot of his time in an Indiana blab school
— children lined up to read in turn verses from the Bible,
placed in front of the class. In many a school it was the only
text available.

A handful of other volumes absorbed the Lincoln boy. Dilworth's *Speller*, first published in England in 1740, appeared
in 1796 in Philadelphia. It taught the alphabet, in simple
words at first and then in complete sentences. Readers also
learned the names of the states in the Union, their capitals, and
rules of grammar. Selections of prose and verse completed the
book. But the lessons also bore moral and religious implications as in the sentences that illustrated words not exceeding
three letters: "No man may put off the law of God" (which
Abraham knew since his mother had told him that often
enough) and "The way of God is no ill way," an equally familiar maxim.

Abraham also acquired a copy of *Aesop's Fables,* in an American edition with morals properly explicated for children in
a free republic. After the fable of the Old Man and His Sons
the editor noted the need for social unity if the Union were
to survive, for "a house divided against itself is brought to
desolation," a moral also repeated in the commentary on the
Lion and the Four Bulls. The Crow and the Pitcher pointed
out the virtues of innovation, whereas the tale of the Ape and
the Fox delineated the qualities of leadership.

Sarah Johnston's arrival considerably broadened the family
library. Webster's *Speller* by far outdistanced Dilworth in advice on social relations, on behavior, on how to choose a partner for life, on respect for parents, and on attitudes toward
siblings. For good measure it contained a moral catechism

and essays on temperance, on the virtues of the Golden Rule, on frugality, and on cheerfulness as an aid to good health. *Robinson Crusoe,* that manual of survival, reinforced precepts derived from other sources by setting them against a wild, unpopulated background familiar to a boy living in the wilderness. *The Arabian Nights,* with its tales of Aladdin and his magic lamp and the voyages of Sinbad, appeared first in America in 1797, under the more edifying title of *The Oriental Morality, or the Beauties of the Arabian Nights Entertainments.* Somewhere Abraham also acquired Bunyan's *Pilgrim's Progress.* The book Lincoln himself later best recalled was Weems's *Life of Washington,* which moved him by its description of the battle of Trenton; he vividly remembered thinking of that glorious cause for which the Revolution was fought at such great cost.

Abraham dearly liked the rhyme and rhythm of poetry. In schoolbooks he read selections from Milton, Pope, Gray, and Shakespeare; but above all the melancholy youth enjoyed the verse of Robert Burns, and he memorized much of it. Burns too was an awkward child, unacquainted with the ways of the world, who worked hard on a small farm, and whose compassionate ne'er-do-well father never succeeded. Burns too pored over the few available books while driving a cart or walking behind the plow, and he too developed a strong distaste for "a situation of perpetual labor." He also suffered from hypochondria, and when he described the rough scenes of Scottish life, in all their beauty and ugliness, he might have been writing about Indiana. This peasant poet articulated commonly shared sentiments in a clear language easily understood. Plain, commonsensical language was a concern of Abraham, who later recalled how irritating it had been to hear grownups talk without comprehending what they said. He pestered his stepmother to explain complicated sentences and would not rest until each thought was reduced to "language plain."

Reading influenced the boy's style of thought. The habit of illustrated discourse remained with him. He learned to weave tales, maxims, allegories, and morals into his conversation, into arguments, and into speeches, not only to strengthen the point he wished to make but also to narrow the distance between himself and his listeners, as if stories understood together created a sense of intimacy.

Bookish maxims, however, did not square with the realities of growing up in Pigeon Creek and offered no clear guide to the goals of life. Often Abraham fell to brooding, sensing the melancholia appropriate to his age and also unease about his future. He worried about whether he would be able to do what he wanted to do, and worried even more about whether he would be able to define what it was he wanted to do. Now and again, as he advanced in age, he tried his hand at poetry, but Indiana, he later wryly noted, was an unpoetic place.

Back-breaking labor was the lot of people as poor as the Lincolns. Young Abraham, always bigger than others his age, soon learned to handle an axe to hack out clearings for the crops. The family planted and reaped corn, wheat, and oats, laboriously using iron-shod plows and crude sickles. There was no escape from tedious chores — grubbing, hoeing, and making fences. The hard earth, still strewn with trunks and stumps, long resisted and yielded only meager harvests. Wild game and the fruits of the forest were staples of the diet until cattle, sheep, and hogs contributed some variety.

Thomas expected his able-bodied, overgrown son to add to family resources and hired him out to local farmers. Abraham dutifully turned his earnings over. For twenty-five cents a day in 1825 he built a strong pigpen to protect a neighbor's hogs from wolves, dug a well, picked fodder among the cornstalks, and whipsawed boards. But he showed no zeal for such jobs and bided his time. He read while plowing (to allow the horse a breather, or so he claimed) and ciphered on boards when no paper or slate was available. He did not envision himself following in his father's footsteps.

"I was raised to farm work which I continued until I was 22," Lincoln said in 1859. Rarely did he express any interest in life on the soil. He knew that precarious existence too well to harbor any illusions about it. Without his father's carpentry the produce of the holding would not have fed the family. Perennial litigation about land titles had driven Thomas from Kentucky. In Indiana too he slipped into debt, on his own account and by cosigning the notes of others. Frequent moves, unrealized hopes, and perpetual instability were the lot of husbandmen in the region. Isolated men and women, removed from the company of interesting strangers and from the outside world, felt closed in with one another. Only occasional trips to the mill or the meeting house broke the monotony; and people unprotected against the environment, sometimes victims of the beasts of the forest and the weather, accustomed themselves to a life of endless drudgery — crude, rough, devoid of amenities.

Abraham knew that other men led other lives. He had earned six dollars a month taking care of the horses and plowing the farm of James Taylor. But at butchering time Taylor got thirty-one cents a day by hiring the boy out to others; and Taylor also used him to operate a flatboat that ferried livestock and wagons and their teams across the creek. Abraham's days were hard and long but also exciting. He slept up in the loft with Taylor's small son but during the day saw Ohio riverboats of all kinds go by to Cincinnati, Pittsburgh, St. Louis, and New Orleans. In the nearby little town of Troy, where steamboats took on wood and other supplies, boatmen, gamblers, planters, and settlers lounged in the street and gathered in Gamage Williams's tavern.

The exciting bustle planted the seeds of calculation. Abraham built his own rowboat and one day got two passengers, pressed for time, to a departing steamer. When he tossed their carpetbags on board, he received two silver half-dollars for his efforts. He couldn't get over it, he told William Seward years later — a dollar in less than a day. He continued this sideline despite complaints that he cut into the business of the licensed ferries. Samuel Pate, justice of the peace near Lewisport, Kentucky, ruled that he violated no statute since he ferried passengers only to the middle of the river, never across. The young man then learned something about how law worked.

A mile and a half from the Lincoln home was an establishment even more extensive than Taylor's, that of James Gentry, a North Carolinian by birth and the big man of the tiny community known as Gentryville. Gentry had bought the store of William Jones, for whom Abraham had also once worked, and also owned more than 1000 acres, a blacksmith shop, and a cotton gin. He too was a reckoner after his own fashion. He knew little about accounting or percentages. But he did know that when he bought an article in Louisville for a dollar and sold it in Gentryville for two, he doubled his money every time.

Abraham liked store jobs for the opportunity to know men like Taylor and Gentry, different from his own father, who seemed never to get anywhere but into debt. The hard work of cutting pork and rendering lard earned but meager wages; the rewards were relief from the farm's drudgery. Customers talked; the weekly Vincennes *Western Sun and General Advertiser* brought news of the outer world; and people with time on their hands came in to tell stories, drink, and sometimes lobby for votes. By way of the new road from Croydon to Evansville travelers, missionaries, traders, politicians, and fortune seekers passed from as far away as Louisville and St. Louis and beyond. Across the counter the young man glimpsed distant vistas of the unknown; and it was on Gentry's behalf he made the trip down river to New Orleans.

Again and again the aimless youth plunged into fits of sadness when the boisterous talk subsided, darkness enfolded the clearings, and only animal cries and the lapping waters disturbed the stillness. On January 20, 1828, a few days before her twenty-first birthday, his elder sister Sarah died. She had acted the mother to him after Nancy's death and for years had been the sole companion with whom he worked and played, shared thoughts and dreams. Seventeen months earlier he had come home from Taylor's for the wedding; watched the arrival of the groom, Aaron Grigsby, son of a neighborhood farmer; observed the ceremony; and shared the infare before returning to the ferry. He saw little of her thereafter. When she died, he sank into a blue mood and long bore a grudge against the Grigsbys, whom he blamed for his sister's death.

Other mysteries of the human condition disturbed the young man. He was present when one of Gentry's boys, Mathew, at the age of nineteen became furiously mad, eyes bulging, mouth covered with foam, throat gurgling, hands flailing at the parents who tried to restrain him. Fascinated by the spectacle, Abraham brooded over its significance and occasionally stood outside the Gentry home in the early hours of the morning listening to the ravings, as Mathew alternately "begged and swore, and wept and prayed." This "human form with reason fled" was a victim of mysterious "pangs that killed the mind."

Always a gangling, big child, Abraham at nineteen was too tall, his arms too long, his feet too big for pants too short. He kept hiding his hands as if uncertain about what to do with them; and that deepened the impression of awkwardness left by an ungainly body. Dark eyes and black, wavy hair set off the unkempt appearance that was the product of rough forest life. Hard work had developed his physical strength and stamina. He could seize an axe by the end of the handle and hold it out straight at arm's length. He swam well and outwrestled and outran most fellows in the vicinity. Yet athletic prowess did not sustain the self-esteem of a man given to poetic introspection. The defenses he erected instead were essentially comic.

Outgoing and talkative, good humored and friendly, he compensated for his awkwardness with storytelling, mimicry, and joking. As a boy, Abraham entertained neighbors by imitating roving preachers and politicians. At fifteen he delivered orations from the tree stumps, to the annoyance of his father who begrudged the waste of time but to the entertainment of others.

Partly deliberately, partly unconsciously, the young Lincoln developed rhetorical skill to gain the approval, or at least the tolerance, of his audience. An immensely popular work entitled *Lessons in Elocution* by William Scott of Edinburgh supplied him with a set of rules for presentation and for the expression of emotions as well as with a handy literary anthology. The book also reinforced his inclination to figurative modes of speech, peppered with familiar stories, folk characters, and tales of common experience. He thus reduced all abstract ideas to human proportions as comprehensible to his listeners as to himself. He treated words and the knowledge they conveyed as actors did, as means of persuasion and conviction, as instruments for manipulating thoughts and emotions.

On the surface he was much like the other lads in the area — more or less hard working and fun loving. And yet he was different in the voraciousness of his reading, in his tenacious memory, and in his insatiable curiosity. He was also moody, given to sharp temper tantrums and extreme vacillations between grief and joy. Though talkative and loquacious he rarely revealed what he himself thought or felt, and preferred to repeat other people's speeches. Shy and deferential, as if unsure of himself in the presence of others, he accepted life as he found it, not knowing what alternative he sought.

In November 1829, while indecision immobilized his son, Thomas once more decided to move. He fled an outbreak of milk sickness in the neighborhood, determined to escape the ravages a previous epidemic had caused. He and his wife received letters of dismissal from the Pigeon Creek Baptist Church, Charles Grigsby purchased their farm for $125.00, and in March 1830 the family was on its way to Illinois where, they had heard, rich, unplowed soil yielded more abundant crops with less work than elsewhere. "Hills look green that are far away" was a common saying.

The journey was longer than any in Abraham's memory. The family, now including Sarah Bush Lincoln's two married daughters, made the 225-mile trip on ox-drawn wagons, Abraham driving one, his father the other. Their ultimate destination was Decatur, Illinois, where Hanks cousins had settled. The first leg of the trip, the seventy-five miles to Vincennes, took five days over uncharted muddy tracks, into which the wheels repeatedly sank. At night the mud holes froze, leaving a thick sheet of ice for the morning so that the weary oxen slipped and the wagons wobbled unsteadily.

Vincennes, a large village, had a blacksmith's shop, a university of sorts, Governor Harrison's mansion on a hill, and a newspaper, the *Western Sun*. The Lincolns arrived on a market day, when farmers flooded the town to exchange produce and gossip, get drunk in the taverns, and make passes at black-eyed girls. The Lincolns did not stay long; eager to get on with their journey, they set off for Lawrenceville, crossing the Wabash River by ferry. Miles of this road stretched through the lonely forest. At other times the travelers moved along busy highways, joined by other families, much like themselves, seeking better lives in the Illinois country. An old Indian trail led from Lawrenceville to Palestine, Hutsonville, and Paradise. The family then crossed the Kaskaskia and arrived in Decatur, in mid-March 1830. The little village, granted a post office a week before, amounted to no more than a dozen log cabins set in an oak grove. Thomas settled west of town in Macon County, not far from the Sangamon River.

A year of hardship and disappointment followed. For months the men labored to clear the wood and underbrush; by the end of the summer they had ten acres fenced and ready for planting. In the fall those who suffered from ague and fevers could do little but shake the affliction out, although the *Western Sun* advised readers to drink an egg mixed with brandy and go to bed when the fits began. The surrounding swamps continued to exude noxious miasmas or "putrid exhalations," and rumors of milk sickness in the area reminded

Thomas that he would never escape that horror, however distant his flight. For Abraham life was as lonely and as desolate as it had been on the Indiana frontier fourteen years earlier.

Then came winter — the winter of 1830–1831, known as the year of deep snow; the drifts piled high against the cabin, the wind swirled through the air, and cattle, deer, and horses sank into deep ravines, to freeze to death or fall victim to the ravenous wolves.

That winter brought to Illinois Denton Offutt, from Hickman Creek, Kentucky, a short stocky man, out to improve his lot by trade and speculation, his eyes open to the main chance like the Taylors and Gentrys of the world. The country was fertile, he believed, but needed markets for the abundance the land would yield. In the spring of 1831 he proposed to send a cargo of produce to New Orleans, "as soon as the snow should go off." He asked Abraham along with John D. Johnston and John Hanks to build the flatboat and navigate the craft for fifty cents a day and a sixty-dollar bonus each if the venture turned out profitably. Lincoln had been to New Orleans before, and this was his chance to leave his father's home. Abraham was of age — independent and legally free to do what he wanted — but he had no defined goal in life except the desire to get away. His parents were by now settled — the cabin built and several acres cleared; they could get along without him. He accepted the deal.

The three men canoed down the Sangamon to Springfield, where Offutt awaited them in Andrew Elliott's tavern. They spent four weeks building the flatboat, then floated down to the Illinois River and along it to the Mississippi. In a month they were in New Orleans. Abraham again proved reliable, hardworking, and earnest, and gained more trading experience.

When he returned, he discovered that his family, despairing of survival in Decatur, had once more moved. Thomas might have gone back to Indiana had not relatives persuaded him to settle in Goose Nest Prairie in nearby Coles County. Abraham visited there briefly but by now had left home. The strange, friendless, penniless boy, as he still considered himself, decided to live for the first time on his own. He was twenty-two years old.

It did not cross his mind to try a city — New Orleans or even Louisville — as some of his contemporaries did. But in April, on the way south, he had passed through New Salem, and he knew that Offutt had secured a retailer's license for Sangamon County. Sangamon was an old Indian word, meaning "the land of plenty to eat." He might as well try there as elsewhere; Lincoln believed himself "a piece of floating driftwood" carried where the current would.

II

Uncertainty

In 1831, when Lincoln returned from his trip south, New Salem was no New Orleans but a scraggly frontier town kept alive by hope.

Wherever settlers came in the West, traders were close behind, fertile in schemes, bubbling over with projects, ready to form companies, partnerships, ventures of every sort. At the rivers' edges they foresaw wharves, warehouses, factories, banks, if only they could assemble the capital, if only the customers appeared. The forest was thick with promoters, every campground a future metropolis.

New Salem, on the Sangamon River, some sixty miles above its junction with the Illinois, was two years old when Offutt made it the base for his expanding business. A grist mill drew trade from the surrounding farms, a store opened on the hill above, and a grocery or saloon stood ready to quench thirsts. The town boomed, its lots laid out and sold, its post office and a small ferry in operation. It boasted a doctor who had come west for his health, with a degree from the Dartmouth Medical School. Soon the number of saloons quadrupled, a cobbler's shop and a tavern appeared, and the town was on the way to becoming the area's commercial center. Only a few scattered settlements were its rivals — Chicago with a population of 100, Springfield with 500. Away from the forested areas the trackless, sun-baked prairie sheltered little else than occasional roving Indian bands.

Hazardous transport impeded the movement of crops to markets. Since high waters in the spring always cut off the poor roads, New Salem's future and that of Sangamon County depended on making the river navigable for steamboats, and that required a large sum to clear it of drifting logs and timber. Still the news, in 1832, of a regular connection to Cincinnati promised prosperity. That year the village reached the peak of its growth. It acquired new houses, a blacksmith, a wagon maker, a second physician, a hat maker, a wheelwright, and a cabinet maker. Its future seemed bright.

The motley population kept changing as settlers moved in, looked around, stayed for a few months, and headed elsewhere. At the height of New Salem's prosperity about twenty-five families resided there in one- or two-room log cabins. Hogs, sheep, and cattle clogged the roads, but fish in the river and game in the woods supplied the necessities of life. The town lacked a church, but the pious gathered for worship in one house or another.

Most people came from backgrounds similar to Lincoln's, although a few Yankee adventurers also turned up. Whiskey flowed freely, to drown disappointments, break boredom, or relieve pain. There was corn to spare, easier to store or transport in jugs than in bushels. Some whiled their time away in wrestling, cockfighting, drinking, and gander pulling. Men of a better sort used leisure in a more educated fashion; in 1831 James Rutledge, Doctor John Allen, and the Reverend John M. Berry formed a debating society. But a temperance club organized by Doctor Allen found few adherents. Mentor Graham, a young man in his early thirties, taught school on a subscription basis — families paid five cents per pupil per day.

Lincoln arrived in New Salem in late July 1831, dressed in blue jeans, rolled up unevenly and as always too short, a cotton shirt and a hat, and nothing else. Since the store did not open until September, he boarded with John Cameron and earned a little money on the side by piloting a raft down river and walking back. When Offutt's opened, Abraham lodged there and fell in with a group of shiftless characters, who spent their free time talking, fighting, and gambling, the only difference being that Lincoln steadfastly refused to drink.

In the winter of 1831–1832 Lincoln found an alternative to the Clary's Grove boys in the meetings of Doctor Allen's more genteel debating society. Abraham called on Mentor Graham for instruction as he plowed through Kirkham's *Grammar* in the hope of improving his language. Jack Kelso, the village vagabond and resident philosopher, who loved to talk as much as he hated to work, chattered on endlessly about Shakespeare and Burns.

The raw community would not let Lincoln relax, however. His employer's instability prevented the young man from settling into a rut. Denton Offutt mismanaged the store, freely helped himself to the whiskey, and grew restless. He itched to move and in 1832 sold out.

Abraham looked for something else to do. Reluctant to go it alone, he purchased on credit a partnership in William F. Berry's general store. A few months later, after ruffians had vandalized Reuben Radford's rival establishment, Lincoln and Berry bought it. But the firm was not cut out for business. While Berry regaled himself with the liquor stock, Lincoln entertained customers and read. Such a combination, as he later said, did nothing but get the proprietors deeper and deeper in debt. The partners tried to turn the store into a tavern, when the county commissioners granted them a year's license in March 1833. Charges of $37\frac{1}{2}$ cents for a meal, $12\frac{1}{2}$ cents for a night's lodging, and $18\frac{3}{4}$ cents for a half pint of rum did not help. The partnership dissolved, leaving Lincoln entangled in debt.

In 1835 New Salem's decline was evident. Offutt had gone. The main tavern changed owners five times, the ferry six. Rumors of the Sangamon's navigability no longer made the rounds, and few new settlers appeared. The dreamed-of steamer turned up but once, only to run aground and sink, and the growth of Springfield cut into the town's trading area, further draining its strength. The stores began to fold, and in 1836 the village ceased to exist. Lincoln's business career ended, leaving him a legacy of court suits to defend. By then, however, war and politics had pointed the young man's interest in other directions.

In April 1832 Chief Black Hawk, violating an agreement reached the previous year, crossed the Mississippi with some 500 braves along with 1500 women and children, intending, he said, to raise corn on the Rock River. The governor treated the sortie as an invasion and called for volunteers. The enthusiastic response sprang from inherited fears of the Indians but also from the welcome restless men accorded any break in routine. Lincoln presented himself for thirty days' service in a militia company composed of friends and neighbors who elected him captain. Few officers of any rank were more skilled than he.

The march began with no clear plan and lasted thirty days, with pigs and chickens along the way the only sufferers. The troops did no fighting, although they sighted one old Indian. At the end of May terms of enlistment ran out, and the company disbanded. Most men went home, but Lincoln, for lack of anything better to do, twice reenlisted at lower ranks. He got no closer to action than discovery of five men killed and scalped the day before his company found them. Discharged at Black River, Wisconsin, he and several comrades made their way to Peoria on foot, then canoed down the Illinois River to Havana and walked the rest of the way to New Salem. His pay was $125 and an Iowa land claim. The Black Hawk War left him the memory of a pleasant profitable outing.

Back in New Salem, the business grind had not gone as well, and Lincoln was at loose ends. He knew everyone in town, had acquired a reputation for honesty, and had proven himself better educated than most. Election as captain had demonstrated his popularity. Equally at ease with the boys in the Clary's Grove gang and with the Reverend Cameron, adept with an axe, a flatboat, or a quill, he was available for the variety of chores the frequenters of Rutledge's tavern asked him to do.

In May 1833, President Andrew Jackson appointed him postmaster of New Salem. Lincoln was far from an Old Hickory supporter, but the place was too insignificant to lend much weight to political considerations. Nor did the young postmaster take it too seriously, leaving the office open and empty half the time, while he went about his own business. The financial rewards were small, but the position expanded his circle of acquaintances. Stuffing the letters and papers into his hat, he delivered mail to faraway farms. And he now had an opportunity to read all the newspapers that passed through the post — its chief bonus he believed. But New Salem's decline brought the happy arrangement to an end. In May 1836 the federal government moved the office to Petersburg, and the position with it.

Of course Lincoln all the while found other things to do. On election days he served as clerk to earn an extra dollar. For a while he became local agent for the *Sangamo Journal* and at the end of 1833 was deputy to the county surveyor. Lincoln knew little about surveying, but equipped himself, on credit, with a horse, a compass, and a chain; he read Robert Gibson's *Theory and Practice of Surveying,* and Flint's *Treatise on Geometry, Trigonometry and Practice of Surveying* and was off on his first surveying job in January 1834. He received in payment two buckskins, which a farmer's wife "foxed" on his pants for protection from briars. Honest, straightforward, and competent, he frequently settled boundary disputes, laid out lots, and marked roads, making new friends in his travels. He now acquired the name Abe.

In the spring of 1834, creditors caught up with him. He had been living precariously, signing notes in the easy frontier fashion. The store was a source of debt, as was the *Talisman* venture, a scheme to run a steamboat up the Sangamon, that came to naught when the promoter disappeared, leaving behind outraged investors. Lincoln was also trusting enough to endorse several mortgage agreements; the bonds he signed as surety made him liable in case of default. Even the surveying equipment involved further credit. Court actions followed and led to unfavorable judgments, so that as late as 1848 he was still repaying New Salem debts.

It was a discouraging balance sheet Abe Lincoln contemplated. He had begun to strike roots in New Salem, but his efforts had borne little fruit. In some ways settled, in other ways not, he was far from having achieved any certainty or sense of purpose.

But, often unwittingly, he was acquiring a role. He talked to people, and they to him — in the store, at the post office, as surveyor in the fields. He was a dependable man to witness a transaction, to assess a value, or to compose a letter. He instilled confidence in his neighbors, for he supplied them with the words they needed to express their thoughts.

Since 1832 he had occasionally contemplated a stab at politics. No doubt he thought himself as well qualified for office as the candidates he had seen and heard appealing for support. There was a thin line between the mimicry in which he had long experience and the stump speakers' earnest rehearsal of familiar arguments.

His first effort had failed. At the urging of Rutledge and other pals in the tavern he ran for the state legislature in the spring of 1832. On March 9 a circular address in the *Sangamo Journal* made his candidacy known.

The twenty-three-year-old hopeful did not have to search for a platform; he found the issues ready-made. Sight of the *Talisman* steaming up the Sangamon had left local merchants visions of corn and other produce going downstream in return for goods from the East. Scarce money plunged everyone into debt. Education was in a sorry state. A proper stand in favor of improved transportation, banks, and schools pleased all, offended none.

Lincoln spent weeks with Kirkham's *Grammar* while he composed his electoral address, which was nonetheless contrived, clumsy, unpolished, and long-winded. He presented himself as a man of the people, appealing to his friends and to those he considered his superiors. Born and still located in the most humble walks of life, he was familiar with disappointments and knew hardship and poverty, yet would make a worthy candidate. He was young and lacked experience, but he could learn. And he promised that if he discovered his opinions to be erroneous, he would renounce them. It was "better to be only sometimes right, than at all times wrong."

Internal improvements, antiusury laws, and better education were the planks of his platform. Having carefully studied the course of the Sangamon River, he pronounced it eminently navigable by steam, after some alterations in its channel (the cost of which Lincoln prudently did not mention). The alternative was a railroad, at staggering expense. Exorbitant interest rates encouraged people to cheat; and no one doubted that education raised the level of "morality, sobriety, enterprize and industry."

These propositions made sense from the perspective of New Salem and Gentryville; and they were in accord with "The American System" Henry Clay had long advocated in Congress. For years Clay had argued that a protective tariff would encourage home manufactures and also provide funds for improvements in transportation, thus tying the nation together and serving the interests of all. Lincoln was a trader, not a backwoodsman, and the congruence in viewpoints rather than common antecedents in Kentucky drew him to the Whig position.

Having rested his case on "the principle of republicanism" the young candidate had gone off to fight Chief Black Hawk. He came back two weeks before the voters went to the polls. A frenzied campaign followed. Lincoln talked to farmers while helping with their chores; he pitched horseshoes with some and wrestled others. In one speech he expanded his platform to include a national bank and a high protective tariff. Tall and gawky, without vest or coat, and sometimes with only one suspender, he looked as rough and unkempt as the electorate and to one bystander seemed yet another loafer with a big mouth and little to do.

Lincoln lost. There were four places and he was eighth in a field of thirteen. Periling one's life in the service of the country — the candidate's lame explanation for his short campaign — was not enough to get one elected. But in his own precinct he gained 277 out of 300 votes cast.

In the spring of 1834 Lincoln ran for office again. There was no presidential contest that year, party lines blurred, and Whigs and Democrats, anti-Jackson and Jackson people, supported him in the race for one of the four available seats in the state legislature. In his capacities as surveyor, postmaster, store owner, tavern operator, and election clerk, Abe had traveled frequently and had visited John Todd Stuart, a rising young Whig lawyer who had encouraged him to try again.

This time Lincoln was cautious. He published no statement of principles. People by now knew for what he stood, and there was no need to test their literacy; nor was there any need to stir the opposition of those who disagreed, by an abstract effort to mobilize his friends. Since the election came in August, the campaign lasted longer and the candidate tried harder than in the previous one. He moved about the neighborhood, visiting Little Creek, Sugar Creek, and other places, attending the obligatory barbecues where all his competitors showed up. He gathered votes while surveying, delivering the mail, and talking to farmers — helping them harvest their corn and listening to their complaints. His personal campaign paid off. He came in second in a field of thirteen.

Reelection in 1836 was easier. By then the experience of his first term and collaboration with Stuart had firmly identified Lincoln with the Whigs, and party lines held faster than before. Abe traveled on the party's behalf to Petersburg (where he promoted the Beardstown and Sangamon Canal) and to

Springfield, where John Todd Stuart, Ninian Edwards, and others lived. To no one's surprise Lincoln announced his candidacy in March 1836. That June the *Sangamo Journal* published his platform calling for universal white suffrage (female as well as male) and the distribution of proceeds from the sale of public lands to the states. Rallies in New Salem and the surrounding areas and addresses in Springfield, Salisbury, and Athens paid off. Lincoln received the highest vote in a field of seventeen. All his Whig running mates were elected. He had mastered the art of successful campaigning.

Legislative service taught the young man a good deal about Illinois politics. In November 1834 the citizens of Sangamon County had also elected him a member of the education convention due to meet in Vandalia, the state capital. Lincoln calculated that he could take in that gathering while he also served his first term in the House. Borrowing $200 to settle his most pressing debts, he paid $60 for a new suit and early on the morning of November 28 boarded the 6 A.M. stagecoach from Springfield. The following afternoon he reached Vandalia, seventy-five miles to the southeast. Clambering off the stage, dressed in the most expensive outfit he had ever owned, one he could hardly afford, Lincoln followed John T. Stuart, who had been here before and knew the town, into a local tavern, where three dollars a day of his legislative salary supported him for the duration of the session.

Vandalia on the Kaskaskia River was then fifteen years old. It had become the state's capital in 1820, when the speculating legislators of Illinois reckoned that the sale of town lots in this isolated, forested area might fill an empty treasury. Reality never matched the hope. The town consisted of a large public square, surrounded by small, ramshackle buildings, several taverns, and two brick state houses. The permanent population of 800 swelled during the legislature's meeting, and since the Supreme Court was also in session Lincoln arrived during a boom.

The representative from New Salem looked on but took no part in the swinging social life of which frequent balls, parties, and receptions were evidence. Elegant ladies made the most of the muddy alleys called streets, and despite mosquitoes and frequent reminders of backwoods rusticity, Vandalia for the moment appeared refined, almost metropolitan. A spirited public meeting sent a few dollars to the nation's capital to help cover the costs of a new statue of George Washington. Colonization, temperance and Bible societies, a bookstore, and the *Illinois Advocate and State Register* were signs of civilization. Lawyers, lobbyists, and office seekers crowded the inns, and taverns boasted an ample liquor supply. License suspensions for "'having permitted disorders, riotings, and drunkenness" were rare. The town, however, erected a jail, with iron bars, a "dungeon room," a place for debtors, and quarters with fireplaces for the jailers.

Procedural matters occupied the first days of each legislative session — choice of a speaker and a doorkeeper (after seven ballots in 1834). Addresses by the outgoing governor and the governor-elect informed the members of the state's glorious future and appealed for better education, canals, and banks. Serious work began with committee assignments. In Illinois many bills passed without referral to committees, which usually met in the evenings when members had other things to do. Still these places were indications of esteem. In his first year in the House, Lincoln received a seat on Public Accounts and Expenditures (the tenth committee in a list of eleven), but at various times served on ten others as well.

The legislature met for about ten weeks and considered well over a hundred measures. In no way could the fledgling member study each of them and arrive at a reasoned judgment, in addition to attending to other duties. Furthermore, the legislature made lucrative appointments. Lincoln could not judge the merits of Stephen A. Douglas's candidacy for the position of state attorney or, for that matter, decide among the various aspirants for the post of penitentiary warden. The sensible reaction was to follow a trusted guide with more experience, in this case John Todd Stuart. On votes to elect public officials Lincoln's record was identical with Stuart's; and on other bills he differed from his mentor in only 20 of 120 cases.

The proposals he himself initiated served the interests of his constituents. He secured passage of a law to authorize the building of a toll bridge over the Salt Creek in Sangamon County; and he supported a bill to increase his county's representation in the legislature.

He lost out, however, on the few occasions when he wished to implement some vague sense of principle. His very first session taught him the difficulty of changing the rules of the game. He proposed to forbid the introduction of new amendments after the third reading of a bill in order to remove stumbling blocks in the way of speedy legislation. He sought to define the jurisdiction of justices of the peace, in order to strengthen local popular control over trials. And he voted against a Christmas day recess. On all these measures he lost.

He failed also on another issue of principle of no more immediate importance. Several Southern legislatures had asked Northern legislatures to denounce abolitionist agitation. Why not? There was little antislavery sentiment in Illinois and much of the population came from below the Mason Dixon line. The gesture of comity was costless. In Vandalia the legislature, by a vote of 77 to 6, condemned abolitionist societies, affirmed the constitutional right of states to permit slavery, and denied that the federal government had power to abolish bondage in the District of Columbia without the consent of the residents. Lincoln was among the six who voted nay. He and Daniel Stone, another Sangamon Whig, explained their position in the House journal late in February 1837. They believed slavery both impolitic and unjust but agreed that abolitionists made matters worse. Congress could not interfere with servitude in the states but, with the approval of the people, could abolish it in the District of Columbia. Though the statement may have clarified his own thoughts, it had no consequences; and Lincoln learned to avoid fruitless pronouncements.

He learned also that in the House other actions mattered more than the few bills he introduced or his services to the Illinois Whigs. He got along well with his fellows, and, as in New Salem, his gift for words helped express the thoughts of others. Lincoln drafted and wrote his colleagues' bills, widening contacts and gaining experience. He came to know the inner workings of the system, as well as some of the state's leading politicians, who remained important in later life. Attendance at sessions netted him several hundred dollars in fees and somewhat less as travel allowance.

In terms of his own life, the most important legislative issue involved the location of the state capital, which the law provided would remain in Vandalia until 1840. Well before then, population shifts reopened the question, and the election of 1834 placed it before the voters. Fully 250 out of 256 New Salemites, Lincoln among them, then voted for a move to nearby Springfield. That town continued to advance its own claims. A series of articles in the *Sangamo Journal* detailed its advantages.

The nine Whigs elected in 1836 to represent Sangamon County in the Senate and the House devoted themselves to the issue. The Long Nine, as they came to be known, included Lincoln, John Dawson (father of ten and a captain in the Black Hawk War), William F. Elkin (father of fifteen and veteran legislator), Archer G. Herndon (a Springfield tavern keeper), and Ninian W. Edwards (constitutionally an aristocrat, who hated democracy as the devil was said to hate holy water).

Before the delegation left for Vandalia, a public meeting laid out the agenda for the people's representatives — state aid for internal improvements, financed with loans not taxes, and relocation of the capital. John T. Stuart, who had run for Congress and lost, came along to help.

When the Sangamon delegates arrived in Vandalia they were

pleased to discover the capital in a parlous state. By the special session of December 1835 the dilapidated state house had already been in danger, its walls sinking, the roof about to fall off, and the Senate floor covered with snow. Having now collapsed, it was being rebuilt but in dimensions clearly too small for the rising membership. The trade-offs began. Every legislator wanted internal improvements for his district, and the Long Nine promised away liberally in return for Springfield votes. Lincoln moved among his colleagues in the unheated corridors and damp rooms, swapping railroads, canals, turnpikes, and bridges for votes. The gigantic internal improvements law, as enacted with bipartisan support, promised something for everyone and prosperity for all at no cost to the taxpayers and with a state treasury ever full. Meanwhile a wolf bill provided a fifty-cent bounty for "scalps with the ears thereon."

There was far less unanimity on the question of the state bank in Springfield. Lincoln delivered a stinging reply to Douglas's attack on it as an unconstitutional tool of a financial aristocracy. The people were not complaining; there was no oppression of any sort. On the contrary, the bank doubled the price of farm products and gave everyone a much-needed sound circulating medium. Opposition to the bank was wholly the work of politicians out to line their own pockets, a group as a rule "at least one step removed from honest men." Of course, Abe hastened to add, these observations did not apply to the fine upstanding men whom he addressed; and after all he too was a politician. But he warned them of "a lawless and mobocratic spirit" abroad in the land, out to overthrow every institution and moral principle that gave persons and property security. The bank guaranteed people enjoyment of the rewards of their labor and deserved legislative support.

The capital relocation campaign now went better than expected. Land officers and state bank directors helped the Long Nine. The Whig Senate got the bill on its way, and Lincoln worked to push it through the first and second readings in the

House, although he could not fend off amendments that called for reconsideration after a year and required the town designated to donate $50,000 to the state. Suddenly a move to table the bill until July and thus quietly kill it squeaked through, 39 to 38. That night Lincoln and his colleagues got tough, cornered hesitant legislators, and threatened reprisals. The act passed, 46 to 37.

It remained to ensure the choice of Springfield over other communities that might advance their own claims. One delegate offered the nonexistent paper town of Illiopolis as a possible site and Senator Henry Mills of Edwards County voted for Purgatory. But on the fourth ballot Springfield received a strong majority and became the new state capital. The chagrined Vandalians suggested a fence around the town to prevent anyone from leaving at the sight of it and argued that Swampfield was a more appropriate name than Springfield for a damp prairie full of bogs and marshes. Unabashed, the victors celebrated in Ebenezer Capp's tavern. As he joined in consuming the eighty-one bottles of champagne, the cigars, oysters, almonds, and raisins for which Ninian W. Edwards paid $223.50, Lincoln may well have reflected how much he had learned in the previous three years — about how to get on with people whose interests differed, about when to take a stand on principle, however little effect that had, and about those conflicts only votes or force could resolve.

Service in the legislature settled his determination to become a lawyer. In New Salem he had already begun to play the role, in speaking persuasively to the townsfolk, in composing their documents, witnessing their transactions, and informally resolving disputes. In Vandalia he perceived what more he had to do.

Law as a subject had long fascinated him. As a boy back in Indiana he had browsed in the state's *Revised Statutes,* and had perceived also the problems farmers encountered in their ignorance of the law. The lack of schooling or of formal legal education did not seem an obstacle. Lincoln had had ample personal experience, more often as a defendant than he cared to think about. He had also frequently served as a witness, attended trials (more amusing than barbecues), and drawn up and signed bonds and other legal documents for his neighbors. John T. Stuart had told him how useful knowledge of the law could be in politics; a career as an attorney would give him status in the community, a steady income, and an end to a life of uncertainty, drudgery, debt, and hard work.

The firm of Stuart and Drummond in Springfield became the library from which Abe borrowed books to read on his walk back to New Salem. He also invested in a copy of Blackstone's *Commentaries* and may have read Chitty's *Pleadings* and Greenleaf's *Evidence*. Many years later Lincoln recalled that those books together with Story's *Equity* contained all the legal knowledge a lawyer needed. Work and practice could fill in any gaps.

Several hurdles confronted the candidate who wished to become a member of the Illinois bar. Lincoln passed the first when he received a certificate of good character from Judge Stephen T. Logan on March 24, 1836. That year Lincoln drew up wills and deeds of sale for his neighbors, attended the circuit courts, and pestered Stuart and Drummond for more information. In effect he practiced law while he read it.

In September 1836 he completed an examination before the justices of the Supreme Court, the second step to the bar. He was not yet a full-fledged attorney but acted as one. In October he appeared before the Sangamon Circuit Court in the case of *Hawthorn* v. *Wooldridge,* filing the plea (signed by Stuart) and writing sworn statements and affidavits. His client lost.

Lincoln took the final step in March 1837, toward the end of the legislative sessions, when the clerk of the Supreme Court in Vandalia entered his name on the rolls. The new attorney then returned to New Salem, but only to pack his bags. He had decided to move to Springfield, where he was a political hero. On April 15, 1837, the *Sangamo Journal* announced that a new law firm, "John T. Stuart and Abraham Lincoln, Attorneys and Counsellors at Law," would practice from an office at number 4 Hoffman's Row, upstairs, above the room where the circuit court met.

He moved most readily who moved alone. At age twenty-eight Lincoln was still a bachelor and preferred it so. Although he was on good terms with women, and especially the safe wives of his friends, he really liked the company of men like himself, rough in appearance, casual in speech, ready for the horseplay of a wrestling match or for a practical joke. Amusing stories, warming drinks, the willingness to risk and struggle — these he associated with masculinity.

He knew from his father's experience that women led to marriage and marriage inevitably entailed the burden of a family. Not only the wife but the multiplying brood, in their incessant needs and drains upon emotions and energies, in effect ended the season of carefree manhood, with its unbounded hopes, its potential for advances into the unknown.

Sooner or later he knew he would settle down, as was expected of him. But better later than sooner. And the pool of possible brides in New Salem was so small as to constitute no visible threat.

Enter a visitor from Kentucky. In 1833 Mary Owen came to New Salem to visit her sister, Mrs. Bennett Abell, in whose house Lincoln often visited. Mary was young, pretty, intelligent, and better educated than most local women. She left a favorable impression on the young man. Three years later Mrs. Abell took matters into her own hands and suggested that Lincoln marry her sister.

Well, Lincoln could think of no good reason why he should not do so. He agreed, and Mrs. Abell, pleased, went off to Kentucky to bring back the bride. But the Mary who returned to New Salem in the autumn of 1836 was not the girl her fiancé had known earlier. She was still better dressed than any women around, but she had grown stout, seemed older than she was, and lacked a few front teeth. Moreover, the rosy bloom of youth had given way to a deep, weather-beaten complexion.

Still, Lincoln had made a promise and he determined to honor the rash engagement. Of course, since he was soon off to Vandalia on legislative business, he had to conduct the romance by mail. The letters to Mary described his gloomy nature and his tendency to deep sadness. They warned what a poor husband he would make — so uncouth and uncivilized. Any girl who got entangled with him would be unhappy. Nevertheless he had undertaken to marry her. Mary's life would no doubt be more enjoyable without him; no woman in her right mind would want him for a husband. But he was honest and loyal, and he had promised to marry her, which he would if she really wanted him. But did she? Really? Perhaps for her own sake she would do better to release him from the promise. Wiggle as Lincoln would, Mary would not let him off the hook. She seemed determined to get married, no matter how discouraging the tones in which he painted the prospects.

When Lincoln moved to Springfield the correspondence resumed. He explained that she had never specifically rejected his offer, but then neither had he, thus far, asked her outright what her intentions were. He went on to darken the prospects of life in Springfield. She would not really like living there. People were haughty and snobbish; she would be poor and, worse, would lack the means to hide her poverty. She was unaccustomed to hardships, and, no doubt for her sake, better not.

But Mary persisted. She liked the idea of moving to Springfield.

The reluctant swain continued to procrastinate and made himself as unpleasant as possible on his few visits to New Salem. To no avail. Mary would not let him go. At long last he recognized the inevitable and proposed.

Mary Owen was no fool. Having forced the surrender, she rejected him and early in 1838 was back on her way to Kentucky. It did not take him long to recover from the wound to his vanity; in a few months he joked about his narrow escape from the unwelcome thraldom and bondage of marriage.

A. Lincoln, as he now commonly signed his name, had much to learn about women and about life. Attorney-at-law, state legislator, and resident of Springfield, he still had no fixed home. When he considered the distance he had come in the six years since he had wandered over from Indiana, he knew that he had been moving fast. But when he thought ahead, he knew also that he was uncertain about where he was going.

III
Arrival

IN 1837 A. Lincoln understood at least that two re-
lated activities would thereafter occupy him — politics and
law. Both involved the application of government to the affairs
of men. Each was his challenge and his opportunity.

In January 1838 the newly arrived lawyer spoke to the
Young Men's Lyceum of Springfield, his subject "The Perpetu-
ation of our Political Institutions," his theme the turning point
at which the country stood. Sixty years had passed since the
American Revolution. The experiment that tested the ability
of a people to govern themselves had endured. The personal
commitment of the founding generation and the passionate
recollections of the conflict, lodged in the memories of the
participants and their children, had sustained the Republic.
Now memories had faded, and ambitious men of genius, dis-
daining the beaten path, might undo the work of their prede-
cessors. Already the orator perceived an ill omen in the
increasing disregard for law and in the growing disposition to
substitute savage mobs for the sober judgment of courts. People who allowed passion to slip out of control acted irration-
ally and plunged into anarchy. The remedy was clear. Let
reverence for the laws become the political religion of the
nation. "Reason, cold, calculating unimpassioned reason,
must furnish all the materials for our future support and
defense."

Two years earlier, in the distant East, Ralph Waldo Emerson

had taken a more benign view of the emotions that he linked with Nature. "The tempered light of the woods is like a perpetual morning" — in the perspective of a town 200 years settled. At the gates of the forest, the knapsack of custom falls off; "Here is sanctity which shames our religions and reality which discredits our heroes." Here "we come to our own, and make friends with matter." Nature even lent a "sublime lustre to death."

Lincoln did not know Emerson's essay, but had seen death with no sublime lustre and had grown up in dense woods shrouded in perpetual night. That grinding life of his, since the moves from Kentucky to Indiana and now to Illinois, had taught Lincoln the power of "the jealousy, envy, and avarice, incident to our nature." Having survived in those dark cabins and rude clearings, he could not deny, only strive to offset, the "deep rooted principles of *hate*." He had seen too much to prattle, in the Concord fashion, of the naturalness of love; and knowing what the absence of law meant, never underestimated its value whether applied to the dealings of one person with another or generalized in legislation. Tasks of both sorts absorbed his attention.

His role in bringing the capital to Springfield earned Lincoln a cordial welcome. The *Sangamo Journal* had hailed the Long Nine as saviors, and to display its new life and energy, the town promptly sent to Vandalia a bond for the $50,000 donation required by the statute.

In spite of its newly acquired dignity, Springfield was still in its infancy. On a site four miles south of the Sangamon River 1500 people lived, surrounded on one side by great prairies yielding but slowly to cultivation and on the others by forest awaiting clearing. Small cabins around the square provided shelter and business addresses for their occupants. Hogs, cows, and chickens wandered unmolested through unpaved streets that were thick with either dust or mud according to the season. The town boasted four taverns, six churches, some schools, an academy, eighteen ministers, and eleven lawyers.

No sooner did a wagon caravan bring the state archives from Vandalia to the new capital than officials grumbled about the high cost of living and the low quality of food. The "Chicken Row" section smelled for miles around, and the boards placed along the muddy streets soon sank into the slippery slime. Francis Simeon, editor of the *Sangamo Journal,* suggested planting rice, the one living thing sure to thrive in the fetid atmosphere. When the legislature met in Springfield for the first time in December 1838, the Senate sat in the Methodist Church, the House in the Presbyterian, and the Supreme Court in the Episcopalian.

In Springfield, nevertheless, people tried to leave behind their frontier heritage and look and behave in more civilized ways. Lessons were available in French, Spanish, and Latin; the Sangamon County Lyceum was a great improvement over the New Salem Debating Society; and the *Sangamo Journal* strained to outdistance the *Illinois Republican.*

No break in political activity followed Lincoln's move to the prospective state capital. The influence of friends, of interest, and of his earlier commitments had attached him to the Whigs. Now party loyalty deepened. Proximity to the center of events and seniority offered him glimpses into the wider meaning of his party identification.

That summer Daniel Webster passed through, escorted by a mounted company, and was treated to a great barbecue attended by all the Whigs in the vicinity. Then for an hour and a half the audience listened, an unforgettable experience. The godlike Daniel informed the assembled that the independent treasury scheme concocted by Van Buren had caused the current depression. The sweep of words opened national vistas and referred to issues of far greater importance than those ordinarily debated in the legislature. But the rhetoric did not clarify the subject. Money was scarce, credit was tight, and river improvements, canals, and railroads remained incomplete.

But the farmers, small-town merchants, and lawyers — among them Lincoln — only vaguely understood the connection to banking and federal fiscal policy.

No more than other legislators could Lincoln sort out the great questions from small, those which involved principle from those concerned with partisan advantage.

In Springfield as in Vandalia, where the legislature continued to meet until the winter of 1839–1840, Democrats battled Whigs with fierce intensity. Among the Democrats was another recent arrival, Stephen A. Douglas, now serving as a register of the local land office and a leader by virtue of political experience and power. Prominent Whig figures were Edward D. Baker, the orator known by a British accent, and Anson G. Henry, a physician of fiery temper, as stubborn as Archer G. Herndon, soon to return to the Democratic fold from whence he came.

In the summer of 1837 a partisan storm blew up around Henry, then candidate for the office of probate justice. A bipartisan investigatory commission suggested by Lincoln cleared him of Democratic charges of padding expenses as one of the superintendents of the new State House construction project. The Whigs then converted victory into defeat and learned the danger of driving the knife too far in. The *Sangamo Journal*, in a series of articles signed by Sampson's Ghost, a pseudonym of A. Lincoln, accused James Adams, Henry's opponent, of spreading the rumors maliciously and vindictively and of being a land swindler and thief to boot. Adams, never before elected to any office, won by a landslide (1025 to 792), gaining support from popular sympathy with his plight as victim of unjust persecution.

Nor was that the end of it. The issue dragged on interminably. Articles in the *Sangamo Journal* under Lincoln's signature branded Adams a fool for his lack of skill as a liar and a fabricator. The Democrat had gotten entangled in contradictions, conflicting testimonies, and layer upon layer of falsehood while prowling about "as Burns says of the devil 'for prey, a' holes and corners trying.'" When called "a deist," Lincoln accused the Democrat of slander, presented himself as a poor humble lawyer abused by General Adams, a high and mighty tory with unbounded aspirations, the owner of land, a house, and a kitchen boy. Adams, twice reelected, died in office in 1843. All that Whig effort came to naught; indeed, it produced results contrary to those intended.

More consequential than such political skirmishes were maneuvers to protect constituents' interests. In the summer of 1837 Lincoln thus attached a rider to one of the inevitable road bills, giving Petersburg the right to incorporation, even though it had fewer than 150 inhabitants. Another measure enlarged Springfield's corporate powers, expanding its authority to collect taxes, extend its boundaries, and improve its streets. Amiable legislators usually cooperated with one another in these matters.

Gains for some at the expense of others made trouble however. No one doubted the need for dividing Sangamon County, then twice the size of Rhode Island. Opinions differed on how. Whigs in the outlying districts and prospective county seats, such as Petersburg and Allenton, opposed the lines favored by the Springfield clique. In 1838–1839 they attacked Lincoln, who had served on the committee that wrote the act they believed did them in. Blistering letters by his good friend William Butler, cosigner of his notes, charged Lincoln and Edward Baker with corruption. Baker replied in kind. But Lincoln had learned enough to turn the affair into a joke. Baker, he explained to Butler, was not responsible for his answer (written while he was distracted by an agonizing toothache). Anyway, no division of this sort could satisfy all; some were bound to get hurt. A. Lincoln would remain a friend in spite of Butler's ill nature.

So, too, Lincoln denied that an increased tax on land soaked the rich. The wealthy had engrossed the state's best acreage and by the laws of justice should pay more than the less fortunate. And, he reminded an abusive correspondent, in a democracy the rich were just too few to carry an election.

Financial issues, rippling out from the panic and depression of 1837, hardened party affiliations. Until President Jackson vetoed a bill to recharter it, the Bank of the United States had regulated the volume of paper money in circulation both by expanding or contracting the amount it printed and also by presenting for redemption in gold the notes issued by banks chartered by the individual states. Once Jackson's action removed that check, the uninhibited state banks set the presses going. Borrowing became easy, prices rose, and speculation flourished. When the federal Specie Circular of 1836 required payment for land in gold, the boom collapsed, dragging the overextended to ruin. The disaster soon affected the rickety rambling structure of internal improvements. Promoters of canals and railroads could no longer borrow funds to complete their ambitious projects; interest payments became due; business slumped; and collapse impended.

Economic problems became entangled in politics. Everyone wanted taxes as low as possible, but people differed on the course they preferred the government to follow in other respects. Small farmers, and particularly those in debt, who opposed the Bank of the United States out of fear that it would constrict credit and keep prices low, tended to approve Jackson's veto and to vote Democratic. Urban artisans who disliked paper money and wanted a lid on prices approved the Specie Circular and also tended to vote Democratic. By contrast, commercial farmers, interested in internal improvements and a moderate credit policy, had favored the Bank of the United States, had condemned both Jackson and Van Buren, and tended to choose the Whigs. By and large, so too did the commercial interests, whether little traders in New Salem and Springfield or big merchants in New York and Philadelphia.

Until 1837 these matters had been remote from Lincoln's

consciousness. Then in April the state bank in Springfield suspended payments, and Illinois could not secure loans for its
internal improvement projects. The legislature that began its
session in December 1838 learned that Illinois had spent $2
million on invisible internal improvements, that the debt had
risen to $15,146,444, and that there would be $92.16 in the
treasury at the end of the fiscal year. Having watched the state
sink that much money into its programs, Lincoln and his colleagues believed it would be foolish to stop; but the financial
mess had to be cleaned up. Bright ideas abounded, but none
were practical. Lincoln proposed that the state buy land from
the federal government at low cost, resell it at a much higher
price, and finance further expansion with the profits. There
was no prospect whatever that Washington would accept the
deal. Lincoln also drafted the report of Archibald Williams, a
Whig from Adams, attacking the Democratic president; yet in
alliance with disaffected Democrats he supported state banks
and opposed a national bank.

Gradually Lincoln began to see that the implications of
questions like the bank, internal improvements, and currency
reached beyond Springfield and Sangamon County, beyond
even the state of Illinois. He had a stake in these national issues as a Whig as well as an American.

Electoral considerations weighed on the minds of politicians
around the calendar, not just on the voting date. Lincoln's
own seat was safe; in 1838, in the race for his third term, he
led a field of seventeen candidates. But though he did well in
Springfield, he lagged behind his opponent in New Salem.
Two years later he won again, but by the narrowest of margins,
for with the growth of the state's population the relative
strength of the Whigs diminished. Lincoln now bore responsibility as a party leader. In 1838, he stood as Whig candidate
for Speaker of the House, but lost because his party lacked a
majority.

In 1838 Lincoln took a personal part in the congressional
contest when he substituted for his ailing law partner, Stuart,

in several debates against Stephen A. Douglas throughout the district. Although the Whig gubernatorial hopeful lost to a Democrat, Stuart edged Douglas out by thirty-six votes. Suspecting that Douglas would contest the election in Washington, Lincoln and Joshua Speed moved to forestall any chicanery. Thinking that minors, people who did not fulfill the residence requirement, and unnaturalized foreigners had added to Douglas's total, they asked editors throughout the state to recheck the tally and suggested proper appointments to precinct committees next time. The Sangamon Whigs were adopting the Democratic political methods they had earlier savagely attacked.

They also adopted the mechanism of the nominating convention that they had once condemned as anti-republican. A two-day meeting in October 1839 elected Lincoln as one of the five presidential electors and appointed him to lead the State Central Committee, with Henry, Baker, and Speed among the other members.

Economic issues became entangled in presidential politics in the election of 1840. To counter the wild charges of Loco Foco Democrats who attacked the state bank and wanted to abandon all improvement projects, Lincoln squared off against Douglas in a number of encounters at the end of 1839.

A long speech by Lincoln, widely reprinted as a Whig campaign document, explained that the Democrat's subtreasury system called for the collection of federal revenue in specie, thus draining away half the nation's circulating medium, to be kept rusting in iron boxes rather than allowed to work. Besides, the administration Douglas supported was without counterpart in its corruption, fraudulent practices, wasteful appropriations, and expenditures. The Van Burenites had boasted that their party's head and heart were in the right place, even if the heel was vulnerable. Yes, said Lincoln, they were particularly touchy in the heel — witness all the Democratic tax collectors who absconded with public funds to Texas and Europe. The Democrats, he thundered, were like the Irish soldier whose heart was as brave as Julius Caesar's but whose cowardly legs ran away when danger came. The speech built up to a gothic depiction of the threat to the nation. Stoked by the "imps of that evil spirit," that great volcano, Washington, and its devilish allies belched forth "a lava of political corruption" that swept across the land with frightful velocity. Lincoln, for one, would resist the tidal wave until the end, "in disaster, in chains, in torture, in death."

Aware that debates rarely turned out the vote, Lincoln advocated the appointment of county, precinct, and section captains and urged a door-to-door quest for support. To Stuart he wrote in a hopeful mood, requesting campaign materials and juicy accusations against Van Buren. Simeon Francis agreed to publish a newspaper for the duration of the campaign. Lincoln, one of the editors of *The Old Soldier,* exhorted all Whigs to buy it, read it, and raise funds. He also thundered against Douglas's organization, which manipulated the post office, an army of 40,000 Van Buren officeholders, "to pilfer letters" and to deprive "old soldiers" of the news that their brave leader, General Harrison, once more asked for their support.

This was the campaign of "Tippecanoe and Tyler too," of the log cabin and hard cider; the Whigs made the most of their military hero and of the plea for patriotism. Lincoln participated fully and earned praise for fearlessly exposing the subtreasury iniquities. Passions rose. Douglas, infuriated by the *Journal*'s nasty comments, tried to cane the editor in the street. But Simeon Francis dragged him off by the hair and jammed him against a market cart. Bystanders pulled the two apart. Francis thought the matter hilarious. Douglas did not laugh — perhaps, Lincoln implied, because he had no sense of humor.

Through the spring and summer of 1840 Lincoln combined law and politics, savoring the excitement of both. Rallies in Jacksonville, Carlinville, and Alton led to visits to other towns where, the Whig press reported, he annihilated all opponents. Debating Douglas in Tremont, he convulsed the house with laughter while vindicating Harrison. The *Quincy Whig* commented that no one could survive Lincoln's crushing arguments as he wended his way north, leaving behind a trail of crippled and broken Democrats. Although the hostile *Register* sneered at "the lion of the Tribe of Sangamon, originally from Liberia," audience approval brought heady satisfaction, as did the advertisement in the *Sangamo Journal* of "Lincoln's speech and Tippecanoe Almanacs."

In June, when the Young Men's Whig Convention assembled in Springfield, hundreds of wagons and horses cluttered the streets. A bystander noted that "the whole sucker state had broken loose." A grand procession, led by a band and by Revolutionary soldiers and veterans of the War of 1812, was prelude to a barbecue, endless speeches, and continuous drinking that was responsible for many a hangover that night. The din continued on into the next morning as the battered Whigs prepared to go home.

Now, with the campaign in full swing, Lincoln set off on a trip to the southern counties. He traveled from Belleville to Waterloo, to Mount Vernon, to Carmi; he spoke, cajoled, persuaded, and slandered. Large crowds gathered to hear him everywhere. Barbecues, parades, flagpole-raising ceremonies, addresses in churches, in courthouses, in open fields, a great debate in Shawneetown, a side trip to Morganfield, Kentucky, a journey to Albion, and three days in Lawrenceville made this a long, hot summer and made Lincoln well known across the state.

The Democrats tarred him with racial slurs; and he and his colleagues replied in kind. If Lincoln came from Liberia then Douglas, according to the *Sangamo Journal*, "devoted to the cause of Africa's sons," went around clothed in "Nigger Wool." Harrison, Douglas charged, was soft on antislavery agitators, but to Lincoln, Van Buren was the incarnation of abolitionism, having voted in favor of free Negro suffrage at the New York constitutional convention. The *Register* called Lincoln a clown, accused him of buffoonery and mimicry, and charged that he misrepresented the views of his opponents. Lincoln called his opponents liars, nullifiers, and aristocrats and rarely missed a chance to list the instances of their corruption or to point proudly to his own humble origins.

Often, the yells and cheers of the crowds urged the speaker to go further than intended. And verbal assaults were the least of it. Frequent fistfights passed without notice, and minor riots with little more. Lincoln the political huckster was in his element. In November Van Buren carried Illinois by a small margin, even though Harrison won the presidency.

The loss advanced Lincoln's education. He had made himself known by traveling through the length and breadth of the state. That in itself had some worth. But he had learned a good deal more than to recognize many new places and faces. He had learned something about the nature of politics.

After 1840 he knew that a good campaign was not a good election; victory on the debating platform did not mean victory at the polling place. The cleverest argument was not the most persuasive. Correctness was not itself convincing. A good organization brought people to meetings; it did not determine what they did with their ballots.

What that meant he already knew, in other ways. Those to whom he spoke were individual human beings, moved by complex impulses and to be neither taken for granted nor underestimated. Greed and self-interest moved them all, but to some degree sympathy also moved them. It did not pay to press too hard, as he had with James Adams. Better, as with Butler, to turn anger aside with a joke.

Often the oblique approach yielded more results than the head-on attack. That was the lesson of his Lyceum speech, which had won widespread approval. His subject had been the threat of mob action to the rule of law. His point of departure had been remote incidents, the lynching of gamblers in Vicksburg, of a black accused of killing a lawman in St. Louis — unexceptionable. But no one in his audience could fail to be aware of an occurrence closer to home, in Alton, Illinois, just seven weeks earlier. Lincoln devoted only a phrase in the middle of the talk to vicious bands permitted to throw printing presses into rivers, shoot editors, and commit other depredations with impunity. Elijah Lovejoy, the editor in question, remained unnamed. He was an abolitionist, and such troublemakers had few friends in a region largely southern by origin. Lincoln knew how little effect a defense of Lovejoy would have; but a talk that patriotically bound the future of the Republic to respect for law explained the danger of unrestrained violence to all his listeners. In the heat of partisan battle Lincoln sometimes forgot the value of the oblique approach to problems, but he learned that he rarely gained thereby.

He learned more slowly the uses of rhetoric. Since boyhood the words had flowed freely from his lips. He had long since mastered the language of personal conversation and the discourse of daily transactions. Expressive stories and colorful figures of speech conveyed meaning to his listeners; and when he faced a crowd relaxed, it was as if he were back at Clary's Grove. But set orations were another matter; laboriously written out and carefully read, the text intruded between him and his audience. Reading, he could not see to whom he spoke; bound to the lines on paper, he lost the freedom to digress and felt compelled to plow on, whatever the effect. Above all, he ceased to be himself when the words dripped out from the point of a pen and formed themselves into high-sounding phrases and contrived constructions, remote alike from the orator and from the audience. He had much to learn before he used in formal speeches the language he spoke without effort.

A. Lincoln also still had much to learn about women and about settling down. When he had first arrived in Springfield, home was the office he shared with Stuart; he had no permanent residence until November 1842.

Joshua Speed, owner of a store in the center of town, dis-

covering that Lincoln did not have enough money to buy a
bedstead, offered him a place. Lincoln climbed the stairs, put
his saddlebags on the floor, and told his friend, "Well Speed,
I'm moved." For his meals he went to William Butler, clerk
of the Sangamon Circuit Court, who took a liking to the young
man and never asked for payment. One way or another he
continued this feckless bachelor existence, living with Speed
and dining at Butler's while in and lodging where he could
while out, riding the circuit to try cases or stumping the state
on the campaign trail. The wounds left by the encounter with
Mary Owen effectively inhibited thoughts of any alternative
mode of life. Besides, he had not accumulated the savings with
which to settle down appropriately. Before long, Billy Herndon, clerk in Speed's store, moved in to make it a snug three-
some.

In the fall of 1839 Mary Todd of Lexington, Kentucky, came
to stay with her sister Elizabeth Edwards in Springfield. Daughter of a well-to-do and prominent Kentucky family, Mary had
found life at home confining and boring. Her stepmother's
rule over a household full of little children created tension and
resentment that might subside in a trip to a lively, amusing
home. Elizabeth's husband, Ninian W. Edwards, was one of
the social pillars of the community. Their imposing hilltop
house was a favorite meeting place, where young and aspiring
lawyers and politicians gathered for balls, picnics, and elegant
dinners. John T. Stuart, a Todd cousin, and other members
of the clan made the family one of the best known in town
and attracted a wide circle of acquaintances. James C. Conk-
ling, Douglas, Speed, James Shields, and others were frequent
visitors.

In this ideal setting, Molly, as her friends called Mary, was
sure to find a suitable match. Young unattached girls were
much sought after in this community, and she was well educated, had been to Madame Mentelle's, spoke some French,
and recited poetry. She loved to dance and talk, was affectionate by nature but also vindictive, and threw her share of tem-

per tantrums — all "feminine" attributes by the standards of the time. The coterie that gathered periodically at the Edwards' mansion considered her a desirable candidate for matrimony.

Lincoln was a regular guest. Ninian Edwards considered him "a mighty rough man" but welcomed this useful political ally to his house. Cousin John Stuart thought well of him, had made him his law partner, and while in Washington entrusted all his affairs to Lincoln's management. Lincoln relaxed when men gathered to discuss political problems, always able as he was to enliven the conversation with an appropriate story. Ninian did not find him objectionable; Elizabeth was polite to this guest, but hardly felt a liking for him.

Lincoln was thirty, Mary almost twenty-one when they first met. He seemed older than he was, ill at ease in the company of young, well-to-do, and well-brought-up girls. Her vitality and charm, her spirited chatter and sparkle dazzled him. He had never before encountered a woman quite like this. But his last affair had been painful, and he had determined not to forget its lessons. Homeless, with no family to speak of, sort of a stray, his background differed radically from Molly's. He still felt insecure and awkward in polite company, a clumsy dancer who did not always know how to behave. They met occasionally, but the summer of 1840 was hectic and Mary soon left to visit her relatives in Columbia, Missouri.

The presidential campaign was in full swing when she returned to Springfield and, along with other young Whig ladies, attended a performance by the Tippecanoe Singing Club in the office of the *Sangamo Journal*. Lincoln and she were also guests at several weddings that fall. Soon rumors spread through the town that Lincoln frequented the Edwards home more than before.

Sister Elizabeth never doubted that Mary was a lady and could do better than this gawky bumpkin, who was far from a gentleman. A number of men hinted at their honorable intentions, perhaps Douglas among them. But disapprove as she would, Elizabeth could do little to alter Molly's preference. Lincoln "loved Mary," who responded to his feelings. The young people continued to meet, went on walks and picnics together (though in the company of others), and saw each other more and more often when the legislature was in session. Mary had found all her other suitors wanting and determined to "marry a good man — a man of the mind, with a hope and bright prospects." Secure in her own social position, she sincerely disclaimed any desire for wealth and sought warmth and protection from an indulgent parental figure, a partner on whose love she could count, whose loyalty would endure, and who would remain sensitive to her wishes. A. Lincoln personified the attributes she valued, and if his background and position were lower than hers, that would only induce him to cherish her the more. At the end of 1840 they were engaged.

For him she filled a need he had not known he felt, but one there since the other Mary had vanished. The campaign comments on his ungainly appearance, his awkwardness in polite company, and his shy unfamiliarity with the Springfield way of the world still plunged him into broody spells. But no longer could he take refuge in buffoonery, clown around with the boys, and turn it all into jokes as he once had. The dignity of office and status at the bar deprived him of those outlets for pent-up emotions. If he found time to put his thoughts into poetry, he did not value the products enough to preserve them; and perhaps the stilted rhetoric into which he cast his formal speeches deprived him of the expressive language with which to probe his own feelings.

Now, at age thirty-one, he sensed a breath of hope. This gay young creature broke through his reserves. In her company he was at ease. Forgetting his lack of manners, he talked to her as he could not to others, on subjects interesting and intimate. She listened and responded, which added to his confidence. Into his drab existence she brought light and gaiety, as campaigning could not. Starved, he gratefully received her affection and love.

Elizabeth and Ninian Edwards, aware of familial responsi-
bilities, sternly told Mary that the match was unsuitable and
would certainly lead to unhappiness. Lincoln's future was dubious, the marriage was beneath the family. The man was a
useful political ally — not potential kin.

Lincoln apparently had not expected such discouragement.
He had hoped that years of acquaintanceship had overcome
earlier social gaps, and as he reviewed the events of recent
months he thought he had cause to believe himself accepted
in the Edwards' home. The rebuff brought back self-doubt.

Yet he also saw the justice of the Edwards' unease. He could
not refute Elizabeth's indictment or promise Mary a life of
ease. No matter how hopeful his future, years would pass before his income would maintain a family comfortably. His life
had been harsh. He was different from the Todds. He could
not be certain of the wisdom of marriage. He ceased to be
sure even of what he wanted.

Devastated, Lincoln sank into a depression that not even
the legislative session's bustle cured. "That fatal first of Jany.
[1841]" marked an emotional crisis. His behavior altered; he
lost his humor, became testy and jumpy, looked and behaved
like an invalid suffused with melancholia. For a week he refused to leave his room and seemed too weak to speak, and
suffered from an attack of hypochondria, which had afflicted
him in the past and would recur.

On the advice of Joshua Speed, Lincoln released Mary from
the engagement. To Stuart he wrote that he was the most
miserable of human beings. "If what I feel were equally dis-
tributed to the whole human family, there would not be one
cheerful face on the earth." Speed was selling the store and
moving back to Kentucky, leaving his friend more alone than
ever. Rumor had it that Lincoln had thrown "two cat fits and
a duck fit," gone "crazy for a week or two." Elizabeth Edwards
rather smugly believed that he had gone mad because "he
wanted to marry and doubted his ability and capacity to support a wife." Lincoln could not long continue in this plight,

neglecting business, disinterested in the news, his mind "in a deplorable state." The next step seemed a matter of life or death.

A. Lincoln forced himself back to the legislature, intermittently at first, then after January 19, 1841, regularly, "emaciated in appearance" but beginning to recover. If he did not feel like writing a long letter to Stuart on the twentieth, he composed one three days later. For a while he considered leaving Springfield. But on January 25, he spoke on a bill to appropriate more funds for building the state house, denying charges of corruption on the relocation of the capital and suggesting that legislators who complained about high living costs could cheapen accommodations by persuading some constituents to come and set up competitive businesses. Lincoln also signed a long protest against reorganization of the judiciary, spoke in support of the state bank, voted against a proposal for a secret ballot, and drafted several other bills. The legislature adjourned on March 1. Since he had decided not to stand for reelection, his career in state government came to an end.

In May a letter from Mrs. William Butler informed Speed that his lovelorn friend was on the mend; and three months later Lincoln came to Farmington, Kentucky, for a happy visit with the Speed family. Peaches and cream ended every meal, and Joshua's mother gave her guest a Bible, the best cure for the blues, which he promised to read regularly. A severe toothache hardly seemed a discomfort.

The two men discovered they were passing through the same emotional upheaval. Lincoln's case, it appeared, was by no means unique, for Speed floundered in an agony of indecision about whether to go through with marriage to his fiancée Fanny Herring. Would he really be happy with her? Did he truly love her? Lincoln's own doubts about whether he would make Mary a good husband fell into perspective. Later letters to Joshua presented a legally tight, well-reasoned case for the affirmative that left an imprint on their author. When Speed reported melancholy forebodings of Fanny's death, Lincoln immediately responded: that very concern was further proof of love. On February 15, 1842, Joshua and Fanny became husband and wife. The parallel was apparent in Springfield.

Keeping busy helped avoid the blues. That month Lincoln, who never drank, delivered a lengthy address on temperance at the Second Presbyterian Church. Intemperance was a personal problem, the remedy exhortation rather than force; a drop of honey caught more flies than a gallon of gall. Reformers would get nowhere without sympathy and disinterestedness. Mere denunciations were ineffective and unjust, for universal public opinion sanctioned drinking. Drunkards were not demons but generally "kind, generous and charitable, even beyond the example of their more staid and sober neighbors." Persuasion could redeem them. A temperance revolution could lead to moral freedom as the Revolution of 1776 had led to political freedom. Both involved the capability of man to govern himself. Together they would open the universal reign of reason in the United States. The *Sangamo Journal* published the talk in March 1842.

The peroration of the speech hailed a future in which "every son of earth shall drink in rich fruition, the sorrow quenching draughts of perfect liberty. Happy day, when, all appetites controlled, all passions subdued, all matters subjected, *mind,* all conquering *mind,* shall live and move the monarch of the world. Glorious consummation! Hail fall of fury! Reign of Reason, all hail! . . ."

At just about the same time that the orator penned those florid phrases, hailing subjection of the passions to the mind and a glorious consummation in the reign of reason, came reassuring news from Kentucky. Speed's marriage was a great success, far better than expected.

That month also, though nothing happened, Lincoln's heart leaped. The first railroad came to town, linking Springfield to Jacksonville. A band assembled; leading citizens got on board and, with a sudden jolt, were off, rapidly consuming the wood supply. In Jacksonville, there were celebrations. Then Lincoln beheld that Mary Todd had joined the group, was well, and enjoyed herself. He gladdened in delight.

It had been a year and a half since the engagement had ended. This diffident couple could not fan it into life again until Mrs. Simeon Francis, wife of the editor of the *Sangamo Journal,* intervened. One summer day Mr. Lincoln and Miss Todd faced one another in her parlor. In those secret ways the heart knows, they agreed and the courtship resumed. Mary defied the judgment of her guardians, and Lincoln overcame his self-doubt.

A hot-weather prank cemented the union. Times were hard; the state banks at Springfield and Shawneetown failed, and the government accepted their notes only at a considerable discount. State Auditor James Shields was therefore one of the less-liked citizens in town. In addition he was pompous, overly serious, and a Democrat, a natural target for Whigs. Letters in the *Sangamo Journal* from "Rebecca," a country woman who lived in "the lost townships," explained why people were angry; having worked hard, they now had no cash to pay their taxes. Her neighbor, Rebecca reported, thought Shields a fool, a liar, and a conceited dunce. Lincoln was the author of the first Rebecca letter; Mary and a friend wrote another. In addition, their poem signed "Cathleen" announced Rebecca's wedding to Shields, as the widow's way of protecting herself against his revenge. When the outraged auditor demanded the author's name, Lincoln stepped forward to take the entire responsibility. Came the challenge to a duel. Lincoln saw no sense to this method of settling disputes and later in life felt shame at his acquiescence. Now honor called; an exchange of notes led to the appointment of seconds. Mediators failed. On September 22, 1842, Shields faced Lincoln on Bloody Island, on the Missouri side of the Mississippi River (Illinois having outlawed duels). At the very last moment John J. Hardin, Mary's cousin, intervened and restored peace, and everyone went safely home.

Mary thrilled to these events as a lady should. The scene at

Bloody Island was the climactic evidence of love. Not only had her swain shouldered the entire responsibility for actions she had shared, but verily he had risked his life for honor's sake. Marriage was the appropriate next step. Lincoln asked Dr. Charles Dresser, Episcopal minister, to perform the ceremony and bought a ring. On the date set, November 4, 1842, Mary informed her family and was adamant when her sister reminded her that she was a Todd. The wedding took place in the Edwards' parlor. A few days later Lincoln ended a letter, "Nothing new here, except my marrying, which to me is a matter of profound wonder."

A. Lincoln had settled down, had arrived at a home— though for a year home was but a rented room at the Globe Tavern, a two-story wooden structure, not much to Mary's liking, but an economic necessity. When the stagecoach stopped, a big bell alerted the stablemen and reminded the couple of their changed circumstance. This was not the setting to which she had been accustomed; and though he had made his financial prospects amply clear, as had her sister, he had assumed an obligation he would attempt to fulfill. The effort occupied the next decade.

IV

Settling Down

LIFE CHANGED. The family head bore obligations of which the bachelor was free.

The love between Mr. Lincoln and Mary endured. In the manner of the times they thus addressed one another and lacked other terms of endearment; but the attachment between them was warmly affectionate. They were not alike in age or habits, and each suffered from personal failings that made conjugal life difficult — he from periods of melancholia, she from occasional headaches and fits of hysteria. But they understood each other well enough to accept spells of withdrawal tolerantly. In other ways they complemented one another — she fastidious about home and his and her appearance, an improving type; he a shelterer, granite-like dependable. The one satisfied the wants of the other.

Later the terms by which they addressed one another changed to Father and Mother, as four children followed the expected sequence of family life. Mary was pregnant soon after the marriage. She went through labor in the cramped spaces of the tavern without servant or nurse and with only a kind neighbor to help. Robert Todd, named after Mary's father who provided some financial assistance, arrived in August 1843.

The Lincolns were poor. Low fees from the law practice dribbled away with disconcerting speed. Lincoln sent small sums to his parents and still had to repay the New Salem debt.

He never worried: "Money, I don't know anything about money." But Mary did, for counting pennies was not in her nature.

Robert's cries soon became a nuisance to other residents of the tavern; in the fall of 1843 complaints forced the Lincolns to leave. They rented a small, three-room frame cottage, where they spent the winter. Then, for $1200 and an Adams Street lot valued at $300, they bought the house of Charles Dresser, the Episcopal minister who had married them. A gift from Mary's father helped out. On May 2, 1844, the little family moved in. Their new home could not compare with the Edwards' mansion, but it was theirs.

Father of a family, devoted husband, active Whig, and solid citizen, A. Lincoln diverged from the norm in one respect. He refused to become a church member, though occasionally it cost him dear to remain apart. The charge of deism continued to plague him, and the easy gesture of affiliation would have spared him frequent explanations.

He believed in something, though not in the forms worshipped by any sect in Springfield. In some crevice of memory, traces remained of the Baptist preachings heard in Kentucky, of the Indiana graveside. On the rare occasions when he reached for an appropriate word, he called his faith Necessity — the acknowledgment, almost fatalistically, of the limits to human ability. Usually his command of language inadequately expressed his feelings. In 1846, when memory,

> Thou midway world
> Twixt Earth and Paradise,

moved him to verse, he commanded only borrowed stylized phrases. Dreamy recollections of loved ones lost inform him half his childhood friends are dead.

> I hear the lone survivors tell
> How nought from death could save,

> Till every sound appears a knell,
>   And every spot a grave.
>
> I range the fields with pensive tread,
>   And pace the hollow rooms,
> And feel (companion of the dead)
>   I'm living in the tombs.

Something was there for which he fumbled in broody moods, but he could not recognize it, which is why he refused to accept any of the conventional appearances religion gave it.

In 1843 Necessity meant supporting a growing family on the fees from a stagnant law practice. Until 1860 Lincoln's income came almost entirely from that source, and from it he maintained a family and financed various political ventures. Had he died that year, his epithet would have been, Judge David Davis said, "He was a good Circuit Court lawyer."

Lincoln preferred not to bother with either abstractions or technicalities. The notes for a lecture on the law revealed how little he had to say on such matters. A good lawyer was diligent, never fell behind in his correspondence, and was able to speak in public. But drudgery was the main part of business. It was better to persuade people to settle their disputes amicably than to proceed through litigation. Fees were important (reasonable ones), and payments at the conclusion of a case were better than large retainers, for that arrangement preserved the lawyer's interest in his work. To skeptics who doubted that any attorney could be honest, there was one answer: be honest without being an attorney.

His comments showed little appreciation for formal study. Whether one read in the office of a practicing member of the bar or independently did not really matter. New Salem was as good a place to learn as Springfield, as long as the books were available and as long as the candidate had the capacity to understand them. Lincoln always studied case by case and, once his partnership with Stuart began, rarely bothered to read a treatise. His business was to settle disputes, not to apply general principles.

As junior partner, Lincoln had borne the burden of the firm's business when his friend and mentor John Todd Stuart campaigned against Douglas in 1838. When Stuart had left on November 1, 1839, to take his seat in Congress, his partner wrote in the fee book, "commencement of Lincoln's administration." Most of the work had fallen to him; he had handled cases, collected fees, and paid bills for wood, a stovepipe, and candles.

In the spring of 1841 that partnership had dissolved. Lincoln had then moved his few possessions across the street to the office of Stephen T. Logan, still a junior partner but with improved prospects. He had learned a good deal from Stuart, but knew he could learn more from Logan.

Logan had been Commonwealth Attorney in Kentucky at the age of twenty-two and had risen swiftly in the Illinois bar, acquiring a reputation for learning and insight. Appointment as a judge had been a signal honor, but inadequate income had persuaded him to resign after two years; and he had built a lucrative private practice by the time he asked Lincoln to share it.

There was a difference of nine years between them, but the gap in experience at the bar was even greater than that. Logan was formal and precise and reread Blackstone yearly, whereas Lincoln was much less absorbed in the profession, not nearly as industrious, and unsystematic to a fault. Logan never succeeded in instilling in him a zeal for money. "Wealth," Lincoln once said, "is simply a superfluity of things we don't need."

But other lessons in the fine points of the law took. Once Lincoln drafted the complaint in a slander case, as he often did, by copying the form book and simply inserting the abusive sentence. Their client, the plaintiff, alleged that the defendant had called him "a damned rogue." Logan, after reviewing the brief, pointed out that the allegation failed to explain why "rogue" was slanderous. The innuendo that the plaintiff was a thief made the sentence abusive, and the brief had not explicitly stated that. Such legal insight was the product of practice, not a skill acquired from books. Lincoln learned to rely less on instinct and wit, more on preparation. He discovered also that knowing the adversary case was as valuable as knowing one's own, a discovery as useful to a politician as to an attorney.

The partnership was unequal. A large share of the fees made Logan wealthy, while Lincoln scraped by. The period of tutelage lasted until 1844, when Lincoln was ready to strike out on his own.

Every respectable firm needed a junior partner — that is, a young man who served not for a salary but for experience, as Lincoln himself had, doing the drudge's work and minding the shop while the senior was out of town, either politicking or riding the circuit. In 1844 William Herndon, just starting at the bar, assumed that role. Lincoln always remained the senior (it was Mr. Lincoln on one side and Billy or William on the other), and there were never any personal relations between them. Lincoln guarded his privacy, his nature secretive and reticent, and the junior never trespassed during their seventeen years together. When Lincoln went off for a term in Congress in 1847, Herndon did the office work and the Springfield business, as he had while Lincoln went on the circuit.

In the early years Lincoln dealt with the simple, basic aspects of country life; ownership of a pig was a hot issue, and disputes over a horse or over interpretations of deeds and documents of sale erupted wherever people had contact with one another. Issues of personal property occupied the preponderant share of his time, again reflecting community difficulties.

Characteristically, he settled his first case as an attorney, *Hawthorne* v. *Wooldridge,* out of court. Illinois was still close enough to the frontier so that people readily took disputes to law, and then just as readily settled them without struggling through formal procedures. Petty controversies over trespass, assault, and the collection of small debts involved insignificant sums; and their resolution depended more on common sense and proper appeals to the jury than on technicalities of law.

Criminal cases were less frequent but more exciting, for the popular drama they unfolded occupied the attention of a whole neighborhood. In June 1841 Logan and Lincoln defended the three Trailor brothers, accused of the murder of Archibald Fisher, who had vanished without a trace. Searches for the body were unavailing. People dug up graves, emptied ponds of water, examined cellars and wells but found nothing. Evidence of a terrific struggle at one spot, the trail of a body being dragged, marks suggesting the passage of a small cart, and two hairs pronounced of human origin were the net products of this effort. But one of the Trailor brothers claimed Fisher's money, and that was enough to jail the three of them.

Apparently cornered, one of the brothers incriminated the other two. Then Logan and Lincoln produced a witness who claimed to have seen the deceased well after the date of the presumed murder. The result was an acquittal. Although Fisher appeared in town soon afterward, "in full life and proper person," some good citizens, Lincoln reported, could not get over the disappointment, having expected a pleasant rope party to accompany the multiple hangings.

Most of Lincoln's trial work was in the Eighth Circuit, a loosely defined area in central Illinois that extended across fourteen counties. Among the judges before whom he appeared were Jesse B. Thomas, Jr., Stephen T. Logan, Samuel Treat, and David Davis, who served until appointed to the United States Supreme Court in 1862. Proceedings were rough and ready. A New Yorker who visited the Sangamon County Circuit courtroom in 1835 observed Judge Logan sitting in a chair tilted back, his ankles higher than his head, a corn cob pipe in his mouth, hair "standing nine ways for Sunday," and attire suitable for a woodchopper. Curious or idle visitors sauntered in and out, all smoking, chewing, and spitting tobacco.

Duties were routine and hard. Twice a year the judge left

his Springfield headquarters and went to county seats to try ready cases. He stayed for a few days or a week in each. Local lawyers sometimes appeared before him, but most litigants preferred the more experienced Springfield trial counselors, who came along with the judge to try cases.

The conditions of travel were a source of constant annoyance. Years earlier Gouverneur Morris suggested that circuit judges combine the learning of a scholar with the agility of a postboy. Times had not changed; in the Illinois of the 1840s judges and lawyers braved fleas, mosquitoes, malaria, cholera, flooded rivers, mud, and sleet. The Eighth Circuit did not travel in the winter, but even in the delightful days of June horseback riding, with saddlebags, across uncharted prairies, was tedious. With lodging everywhere primitive, lawyers slept two to a bed, and criminals and judges often ate at the same table. Lincoln did not mind the hardships, although he too referred to the tedium. But the circuit was a vital part of his life and also had a political function, since he gathered here the backing he needed for statewide leadership.

In April of each year he set forth on the circuit, half glad to be out of Springfield and away from his perennial personal difficulties. A nag carried him from town to town, along empty trails, to warm receptions in little communities — Tremont, Danville, and Charleston, where court days were a welcome diversion.

On the circuit people met and formed alliances, exchanged local news, and estimated political prospects. Traveling in the company of other lawyers and judges, Lincoln observed future rivals or allies at close quarters. The camaraderie among the brothers of the bar transcended professional differences. Sharp contests and bruising debates taught lessons in self-control, and also in manipulation and maneuver. A professional attitude enabled a man to take matters in stride and prevented disputes from degenerating into personal quarrels. Tact, patience, and generosity were essential if this grueling existence were not to destroy self-control. Lincoln learned how to argue without be-

coming vindictive, abusive, or embittered — important lessons
for a debater.

There never was time properly to prepare a case, for often
the local attorney or the client chose counsel from the circuit
bar only when the retinue came to town. Trials were therefore
rapid, with no indulgence for legal pyrotechnics. Lincoln
manifested his skill chiefly in handling the jury; he often
yielded on technical questions, even when friendly opponents
suggested he defend his point. Lincoln was at his best when
addressing the jury; he was always aware of the importance of
making his argument comprehensible to the twelve men before
him. They were not substantially different from the people he
had known in Indiana, New Salem, and Springfield. Having
met them on their own terms, he understood their character
and always reduced the complexity of his exposition and illustrated his speech with familiar tales, full of wit and delivered
in a homely style. Simplicity was his strongest point. An agent
who collected the pension due the widow of a Revolutionary
War veteran ($500) kept half the amount. Lincoln sued on
the ground that the fee was excessive. For his address he made
the following notations: "No contract . . . Unreasonable charge
. . . Revolutionary war. Describe Valley Forge privation. Ice.
Soldiers' bleeding feet. Plaintiff's husband. Soldier leaving
home for army. SKIN DEFENDANT. Close." The judicious mixture
of appeals to equity and sentiment swayed many a jury.

Lincoln served primarily as a trial lawyer; his litigation
dealt with property disputes, simple contracts, and similar
daily issues rather than with banks, incorporation, or railroads.
His firm engaged in one-fifth to one-third of all Springfield
cases, and that accounted for almost his entire livelihood. Lawyers commonly dabbled in outside money-making activities,
but not he. His real estate holdings were always small; and he
rarely stopped to make an extra dollar by dealing with matters outside his domain. When asked to take on other business
Lincoln answered that he could not undertake it: "As to the
real estate, we can not attend to it, as agents, and we therefore

recommend that you give the charge of it, to Mr. Isaac S. Britton, a trust-worthy man, and one whom the Lord made on purpose for such bussiness [sic]."

In the 1840s he served many five- and ten-dollar clients, and throughout his practice twenty dollars was a good fee, one hundred dollars a large one. Payment often came in produce, goods, or livestock rather than in cash. But he was a persistent collector; unwilling to take advantage of anyone, he would not allow others to do him in. His annual income amounted to about $2000 in the 1840s and remained about the same in the 1850s. However, boring details did not interest him. Sloppy accounting and bookkeeping and misplaced correspondence showed that he never developed a sharp business sense. Nor did fine legal points concern him. "If I can free this case from technicalities and get it properly swung to the jury, I'll win it," he often said.

From the humdrum routine of domestic life and petty lawsuits, politics was an escape. Mary bore him three more sons — Eddie in 1846, Willie in 1850, and Thomas in 1853. Eddie died at the age of four; for the others life in Springfield unfolded uneventfully. Their father watched the passing years, somberly, broodingly. Lincoln still tried his hand at poetry, though few hints of emotion showed through the stilted lines. In an account (1846) of a bear hunt, the dogs dispute the prize and

> . . . how to trace
> What's true from what's a lie
> Like lawyers, in a murder case
> They stoutly *argufy.*

The most aggressive earns the poet's salute:

> Conceited whelp! we laugh at thee —
> Nor mind, that not a few
> Of pompous, two-legged dogs there be,
> Conceited quite as you

A trace of feeling animated the verses (1846) on Matthew Gentry, a bright lad, and the son of the rich man in the old neighborhood, now

> A human form with reason fled,
> While wretched life remains.

Recollection of a visit in 1844 to the old home and to the grave of Nancy Hanks two years later evoked a shy apostrophe:

> O death! Thou awe-inspiring prince,
>   That keepst the world in fear;
> Why dost thou tear more blest ones hence,
>   And leave him ling'ring here?

The iron rule of Necessity could not explain everything to a lawyer, no longer young, now approaching the age of forty.

Politics, on the other hand, dealt in certitudes, arraying as it did right against wrong. Politics also was life. It involved people in exciting contests, which left losers behind but rewarded winners with real prizes, not with a bear hunt's worthless pelt.

Withdrawal from the legislature by no means marked the end of Lincoln's political activity. Always an active partisan, he found the staple of conversation, the ever-renewed source of debate, in the Springfield courthouse and on the circuit. His own neighborhood, peopled largely from Kentucky, remained solidly Whig. But Illinois, growing by the years as the northern counties filled up with migrants from other parts of the country, had voted Democratic in 1840 and could go either way in 1844.

The Whig convention in Baltimore nominated Henry Clay for the presidency on May 1, 1844. In Illinois Clay clubs sprouted; celebrations whipped up enthusiasm; rallies expressed support; and Lincoln made the circuit a campaign trail, working hard both from conviction about the correctness of "Harry's" policies as well as from fellow-feeling for the Kentuckian.

The *Illinois State Register,* Democratic as in the past, venomously dubbed Lincoln "the jester and a mountebank," a "long legged varmint" who could "make a speech which is all length and height like himself but no thickness." Insults spurred him on. In Virginia, Illinois, Lincoln portrayed "the absurdities of locoism and the soundness of Whig principles." In Sugar Creek, Rochester, and Jacksonville he tried to convince farm audiences that a high tariff made goods cheaper. In Peoria, 8000 people turned out to listen. Lincoln's addresses varied with the circumstances, but the constitutionality of the bank and Democratic difficulties over the annexation of Texas were constant. In June the Illinois Whigs had to fend off Democratic charges arising from nativist riots in Philadelphia. Lincoln argued defensively that his party was not anti-Catholic or opposed to foreigners, that it favored reasonable naturalization laws and supported the freedom of all to worship as they pleased.

In July the Sangamon Whigs left town with a band, a glee club, and banners on their way to a three-day rally and barbecue in Vandalia. Yet another band met the delegation on its return and escorted it to the Clay cabin, where Lincoln spoke. Spirits were high, although a tall flagstaff, called a Liberty pole, killed a loyal Whig helping to hoist it up. A few hotheads charged the Democrats with engineering the accident, and when the workmen hired to erect the pole became sick after drinking from a public well, the opposition were suspected of poisoning the water. Only later did it emerge that a boy had accidentally dropped a packet of fly salve for horses into the well. Banners, flags, glee clubs, and bonfires and fireworks restored good spirits.

Lincoln spoke at a mass rally in Decatur and debated in Peoria. In October he traveled to his boyhood home in Indiana, talked at the old brick schoolhouse in Bruceville and under a large elm in Washington, visited Rockport and Gentryville, and received a warm welcome in Evansville.

In November Clay carried central Illinois, but Polk won the

state and the nation, although the popular vote was extremely close. A letter from her stepmother informed Mary how Clay received the news. At a wedding reception in Lexington, Kentucky, he opened the message informing him of the frustration of his lifelong ambition. For a while he stood frozen, his face ashen, but soon he recovered his composure and joined the celebration. It was clear to all that the gallant Harry of the West had fought his last presidential battle.

President Tyler interpreted Polk's victory as a mandate for expansion and promptly secured the annexation of slaveholding Texas. Therewith he removed the stopper that had safely confined the explosive issue of territorial expansion. Almost without exception, Americans of every party and section believed that their form of government would spread in the future across the continent, the hemisphere, and indeed the world. But they did not all believe that the process required expansion of the boundaries of the United States — particularly not at the cost of increasing the number of slave states.

Unaware of the consequences, Springfield Democrats celebrated with a torchlight parade and booming guns. At the head of one procession, hanging neck down from a gallows, was a dead Clay raccoon; above it crowed a live Polk rooster. The town had earlier affirmed the unquestioned right of the United States to the whole Oregon territory and had favored immediate annexation of Texas. Equivocal stands on both issues had hurt the Whigs.

The results discouraged many, including Lincoln, who perceived the outcome as an indictment of splinter parties, which not only failed themselves to achieve their goals but also frustrated the attempts of others to attain them. The Liberty men, including deluded Whigs who favored freedom in the territories and regarded the annexation of Texas as a scheme to extend bondage, had blindly sacrificed the possible good and had contributed to a certain evil out of a mistaken notion of right and wrong. A mere 6000 votes had given New York State and therefore the presidency to the Democrats. The election of

Clay would have curbed the spread of slavery; the desertion of the Liberty people had led to Polk's victory and its expansion. No doubt they were sincere in their opposition to slavery, which they had unwittingly strengthened. Still, Lincoln recalled, "By their fruits ye shall know them." For the moment, however, Texas was not crucial; with no other space into which to expand, the South's peculiar institution would die a natural death.

With the presidential election out of the way, Lincoln applied his energies to his own political future. His eye had long rested on the seat in the federal House of Representatives once held by John Todd Stuart.

The Seventh Illinois Congressional District was solidly Whig, with nomination tantamount to election. The officeholder had to be away from home and business much of the year; life in Washington was unpleasant; and junior congressmen rarely found an opportunity for achievement. Still this was one of the few positions that made a man known outside his own county, and Lincoln wanted it — at least for a term.

In February 1843 he had written friends of his interest in the seat and had tried to gather support. There were then two other aspirants, John J. Hardin, Mary's cousin from Morgan County, and Edward D. Baker. Lincoln was not even the choice of his own county delegation to the convention in Pekin, alienated by slanderous accusations that he was a deist, a duellist, and "the candidate of pride, wealth and aristocratic family distinction." The convention designated Hardin in a show of unanimity, with the understanding that Baker would be the next candidate and that Lincoln would follow two years later. Feeling much like the groomsman to the man marrying his dear "gal," Lincoln wrote Hardin letters of support and even wagered that the winning Whig margin in Sangamon would be larger than in the candidate's home county of Morgan. He won that bet at least, as Hardin gained the seat, which then passed to Baker as per the agreement.

Lincoln's turn was next. In the summer of 1845, while on the circuit, he began to call in his debts, assuring himself of party support. In November his letters emphasized that "Turn about is fair play." Tabulating possible support, he pronounced himself hopeful and notified friendly editors of his intentions. Taking nothing for granted, he also worked hard to make sure that voters understood what was at stake, and he planned a trip through the more doubtful counties once the Supreme Court in Springfield had adjourned. Meanwhile he sought pledges from various Whig leaders.

Hardin, restive, proposed that the party discard the convention nominating system and adopt a new method, more favorable to him. Lincoln indignantly declined: It was his turn now. Hardin suggested that no one campaign outside his own county. Lincoln refused: Having been in Congress, Hardin was better known than he. Hardin, dissatisfied with Lincoln's "improper manner" of seeking the nomination, accused him of adopting the hated Democratic principle of office rotation. Lincoln talked of "mutual concessions for harmony's sake." But privately he reminded Hardin of the agreement, charged him with disrupting party unity, and expressed the hope that he would "think better and think differently of this matter" in the future. In mid-February 1846 Hardin withdrew from the race; the party managers by then had accepted the validity of Lincoln's claim. It was indeed his turn.

Two weeks after the party convention nominated Lincoln (May 2, 1846), the United States was at war with Mexico. Hardin, a brigadier general in the Illinois militia, volunteered for active duty. Baker resigned his congressional seat and hurried home to recruit a regiment. Military companies paraded the streets of Springfield, and the governor, Lincoln, and others urged a large crowd to uphold the national honor. Men volunteered, cadets drilled, and fighting fever swept the town. The Fourth Illinois assembled and moved first to Alton, then to St. Louis, where its blue uniforms and glazed oilcloth caps impressed everyone favorably. In mid-August the regiment reached the Rio Grande, and the glorious adventure turned into a mess. Torrid climate, poor food, polluted water, forced marches, and unsanitary conditions decimated the ranks. Two months later only 400 of the 770 men who left Springfield were fit for duty.

Meanwhile the electoral campaign went on. Once more Lincoln answered the charges of infidelity by affirming his belief in the Bible and in the controlling force over man's mind that he called Necessity. The rumor of infidelity may have emanated from Peter Cartwright, the well-known Methodist preacher who was his Democratic opponent. That August Lincoln received 6340 votes to Cartwright's 4829, an unprecedented majority.

A life heretofore confined to the small Illinois corner of the stage now spread out across the national scene, in a fashion no one had foretold.

A period of waiting intervened. Because the federal year began in March, a lame duck Congress sat in the winter of 1846–1847. Lincoln did not actually take his seat until more than a year after his election. The interval he spent in preparation and in winding up local affairs. In the spring of 1847 he made the circuit again and chaired a committee to arrange ceremonies for the Illinoians who had died in the war, among them his late antagonist, John J. Hardin. Lincoln also worked to persuade the Springfield folk to subscribe to a railroad to Alton and set an example by himself purchasing two shares for $200.

Under Mary's direction the congressman-elect bought new clothes, including a black coat and trimmings and a $1.25 pair of suspenders. An observer did not find the results as elegant as Mary had hoped. Lincoln was "tall, angular, and awkward, he had on a short waisted, thin swallow tail coat, a short vest of the same material, thin pantaloons scarcely coming to his ankles, a straw hat and a pair of brogans with woolen socks."

In July a national river and harbor convention drew him

to Chicago, a city of increasing size and importance. Not since the visit to New Orleans almost twenty years earlier had Lincoln felt the throb of urban growth. Beef from a new slaughter-house readied for export to England, farm produce pouring into thriving markets, and a boom in building along the wide shores of Lake Michigan were evidence of vitality. In 1832 about 100 people huddled around Fort Dearborn; in 1847 the population approached 30,000. An area the size of one square mile expanded to include the surrounding nine square miles.

Center of a rich agricultural region, at the junction of the newly dug Illinois and Michigan Canal with Lake Michigan, Chicago was the future hub of east-west railroad passage. The city was acquiring a cosmopolitan character with the successive waves of Irish, English, and German immigrants, with three bathhouses, several hairdressers and tonsors, ice cream parlors, groceries, and wine merchants. Ceaseless activity pervaded the place. Roads of mud and dust were as bad as elsewhere, filth littered the area, and offensive smells arose from faulty drainage and the carcasses of dead animals. Hogs and cattle preempted the sidewalks, and weekly wolf hunts in the nearby countryside were a favorite pastime. But new buildings replaced the old frame houses spattered with mud, hotels and coffee houses sprouted, and grog shops catered to the thirsty.

Delegates to the convention poured into town for weeks, finding accommodations in private homes, taverns, and ships in the harbor. Parades and bands greeted the newcomers. New York sent 300 delegates, among them Horace Greeley and Thurlow Weed; but Illinois had the largest contingent — 1016. In all about 20,000 visitors swamped the city, as the East and the West united in the support of internal improvements.

Both parties were present at the meetings that began on July 5, 1847, but the Whigs were in control. David Dudley Field of New York set forth the strict constructionist argument favoring only improvements consistent with the limited powers of the federal government; Lincoln answered "briefly and happily" as the *New York Tribune* reported. A committee of the whole, chaired by Greeley, adopted a resolution in favor of a railroad to the Pacific, which Lincoln supported.

Lincoln, though certainly not prominent, was becoming known. The *Chicago Journal* took note of his presence. "We know the banner he bears will never be soiled." And on the way back the *Boston Courier* correspondent, J. H. Buckingham, shared the stagecoach with him between Peoria and Springfield. The reporter was amazed at how many people the congressman knew. "Such a shaking of hands — such a how-d'ye do — such a greeting of different kinds . . . was never seen before." Lincoln had a kind word, a smile, and a bow for everyone on the road, even for "the horses, and the cattle and the swine."

The amiable congressman, in transit, left a meeting that expressed sentiments thoroughly in accord with those of Henry Clay, in favor of development of transportation to bind the expanding nation together. In Washington, Lincoln, ever an admirer of the aging Kentuckian, would see the eruption of an issue Clay had always dreaded, that of slavery's future.

V

Necessities

In October 1847, the Lincolns rented their home for ninety dollars a year and, with the boys, left for Washington, on the way meeting Speed in St. Louis, and staying for three weeks with Mary's family in Lexington.

In Springfield Lincoln had known Billy the Barber (William Fleurville), among other free blacks, and images of colored people among the strange sights of New Orleans may have left fleeting memories. But in Lexington came the first prolonged exposure to slavery. The house slaves, almost part of the family, differed from the hands who manned the Todd cotton mills outside town. Wartime, with many men absent and petty pilfering and lawlessness common, spread a vague sense of foreboding among the whites, heightened by the trial of several slaves for attempting to poison their masters and by newspaper advertisements for runaways. Near the Todd house stood an auction block and a jail, where one day Lincoln saw the slaves of John A. Leavy sold to satisfy a judgment obtained by Todd.

Henry Clay, mourning for his son killed in the war, spoke on November 13 in the Lower Market House. Lincoln attended. Having come to the autumn of life, Clay argued that the war was not one necessary for defense "but one unnecessary and of offensive aggression." Mexico, not the United States, was protecting her firesides, her castles, and her altars. Lincoln also heard Clay repeat his view on slavery — a great evil, but for the time "an irremedial wrong to its unfortunate victims." The listening congressman perceived, although he did not fully understand, the connection between war and slavery.

The Lincolns arrived in Washington late on December 2, 1847. For a few nights they roomed in a hotel, then found cheaper, permanent quarters in widow Ann Sprigg's boarding-house.

The capital was "an ill contrived, ill arranged, rambling, scrambling village," its houses surrounded by privies, pigsties, and goose pens. Piles of garbage littered the streets; hogs and cows scavenged the alleys. Elegant dwellings mingled with shanties. Although residents of the District could boast of their two paved streets, coaches avoided Pennsylvania Avenue alto-gether to spare passengers the unbearable jolts from the un-even big cobblestones. Above the Capitol rose a wooden dome, but most government departments made do with small two-story buildings. Gangs of slaves in chains attracted little no-tice. Gambling places did a brisk business while Congress was in session, and many a grocery thrived. Abundant produce and farm goods came in from nearby Maryland farms. Other shops existed, but for serious and better purchases people went to Baltimore, about two hours away by rail.

Street lights illuminated Pennsylvania Avenue, but only when Congress met. Fifteen policemen with one captain did duty during the day, none at night. The city boasted thirty-seven church buildings belonging to eight denominations, as well as two newspapers, the *National Intelligencer* (Whig) and the *Washington Union* (Democratic) — and an Abolitionist sheet, the *National Era.* Men far outnumbered women since few congressmen brought their wives, and a transient popula-tion of officials, office seekers, and legislators alternately swelled and decreased the population.

Polk's austerity and temperance infused White House social life — there was no dancing and little alcohol. Secretary of

State James Buchanan entertained more extensively; he was host on one occasion to 1500 guests. President Madison's widow and Mrs. Alexander Hamilton were among the notables. Most people dined at five, although the British ambassador waited until six, when his richly dressed liveried servants arrived with dinner on massive silver platters.

Mrs. Sprigg's boardinghouse, on Capitol Hill, catered mainly to Whigs. Other occupants later remembered Lincoln's dinner stories, which began "Now that reminds me..." Lincoln enjoyed a nearby bowling alley, covering his ineptitude with the usual good humor. Sometimes he and Mary listened to the Marine Band perform on the White House steps. Few more exciting events animated the life of a new congressman.

Just before Christmas of 1847, the freshman from Illinois introduced a resolution questioning the veracity of the president. Polk had asserted that invading Mexicans who shed the blood of American citizens on American soil had compelled him to declare war. Lincoln asked, where?

That summer Whig generals had been winning battles while the nation prepared to decide whether the vast new areas victory would bring should be slave or free. The issue threatened party unity. A year earlier Congressman David Wilmot's antislavery proviso to an appropriations bill had opened a sectional cleavage in the Whig ranks, and the Democrats felt similar pressure.

The sense of impending internal conflict called attention to the reasons why the United States had gotten into the war in the first place. A Clay man, dubious about Texan annexation, Lincoln smelled a conspiracy. Where, he asked, was that spot on which Polk had said armed invaders had attacked innocent Americans without provocation?

Lincoln added little to the charges earlier leveled against Polk by Clay and other Whigs, and neither the president nor anyone else in Washington paid much attention to the resolution. To reinforce his case Lincoln on January 12, 1848, carefully presented the evidence to the House in the best legal fashion, concluding that Polk's lies had led the United States into an unwarranted war. The blood of Abel cried to heaven against the Cain in the White House. Lincoln also supported a resolution introduced by George Ashmun of Massachusetts declaring that Polk had "unnecessarily and unconstitutionally" begun the war. Polk ignored it all.

Once more Lincoln learned the futility of a frontal attack based on pure principle, and the danger to a leader who moved too far ahead of his followers. The reaction back home to his votes and speeches convinced him that he had better mend fences or lose all hope of support. During the remainder of his term Lincoln took no clear stand on slavery in the territories or in the District of Columbia, and when the question arose he cast votes that could be interpreted either way. He patiently explained to Herndon that both he and the Whigs in Congress had always supported the army and had provided the soldiers with everything needed to fight the war. To convince the folks in Springfield, Lincoln sent back copies of the *Congressional Globe* and the *National Intelligencer,* his own speech and the addresses of other Whig leaders — Joshua Giddings of Ohio, Alexander H. Stephens of Georgia, and Robert Toombs of Georgia.

Nothing helped. The *Illinois State Register* charged him with disloyalty and duplicity in an editorial, "Out Damned Spot." Although the *Sangamo Journal* (now renamed the *Illinois Journal*) came to his defense, the Democrats ridiculed his "imbecile and silly" stand, branding him upholder of "the guerilla bandito [Santa Anna] that draws his weapon reeking with the blood of our assasinated countrymen." A public meeting in Morgan County denounced "slanderers of the President, defenders of the butchery at the Alamo, traducers of the heroism at San Jacinto." Lincoln had disgraced the Seventh Congressional District by heaping "infamy on the living brave and illustrious dead." The name "spotty Lincoln" spread across the state.

Reappraising his situation, Lincoln decided neither to run again nor to justify himself publicly. A congressman's life had not been to his taste or to that of his wife. In April 1848 Mary left Washington with the two boys and went to stay with her family in Lexington. Lincoln missed her. Their room at the boardinghouse seemed lonely, and he lost all zest for work. He worried about her headaches, her weight, and about whether she had enough help with the children. Mary replied reassuringly: No, the children had not forgotten their father. Eddie suffered from "a little spell of sickness" but would soon be well. Bobby had brought home a kitten, and its prompt ejection had provoked screams and tears. She missed him as much as he missed her. Lincoln answered in a fond, paternal tone that a reunion would delight him, but she had to promise to be "a good girl." He also asked Mary about two bills that arrived after her departure (when she had assured him that she had taken care of all debts).

Rather than remain in Washington, Lincoln preferred to use his position as leverage for acquiring a rewarding appointive office. The task at hand was to elect a Whig president for the sake of principle and for a personal chance at the spoils. Only a nominee who would attract Democratic and independent voters could win; and Harrison's victory in 1840 had demonstrated the attractiveness of a military hero. Lincoln joined the Young Indians, an informal gathering of congressmen, Toombs and Stephens among them, who favored Zachary Taylor, about whose presidential stature Lincoln had doubts. But Taylor alone could bring together the votes of barnburners, native Americans, Tyler men, disappointed office-seeking locofocos and the Lord knows what; and such a combination was bound to win. The Whig convention in Philadelphia nominated Taylor and prudently published no platform. The candidate limited himself to ringing endorsements of the Constitution of the United States and peace, prosperity, and Union.

Lincoln hit the campaign trail. Orders went to Herndon in

Springfield: Organize. Form Rough and Ready clubs, have meetings and speeches, attract the shrewd and wild boys around town (whether just of age or a little under age did not matter). Lincoln recalled that when he was young he had not waited to be hunted up and pushed forward by older men. He never would have gotten anywhere had he sat back. Evening meetings drew greater attendance and would not only help elect Old Zach but would give the lads an interesting pastime. When Herndon complained that the old leaders blocked his advancement, Lincoln, by now himself classified as an old man, gave William the facts of life. Only hard work would get him ahead.

Lincoln spent June and July 1848 in Washington because Congress was in session. But the floor of the House saw less of him than did party headquarters. He advised Horace Greeley on strategy and suggested that Taylor let the bank issue rest. Lincoln defended internal improvements against Democrats who seemed to believe, Do nothing at all, lest you do it wrong.

In support of Taylor, in opposition to the Democrat, Lewis Cass, he delivered on the floor of the House in July a speech with all the flavor of stump oratory.

Taylor, like Jefferson and other true American statesmen, believed in the sparse use of power, Lincoln said. For those who charged that Old Zach lacked any principles, the speaker listed several, though none too clearly; but then the Cass position on many issues was equally cloudy. In any case, readiness to follow the will of the people as expressed in Congress was as principled as one could get. It was clear as noonday that principles applied in the drafting of legislation were not in the presidential domain but the prerogative of the Congress. Hence Taylor's failure to speak about principles was inconsequential.

On the other hand, Cass's inconsistency had clearly shown the lack of principles. The Democratic idea of writing a platform and then forcing everyone to accept it was wrong; and anyway, the people were voting not for principles but for a president.

Lincoln then added a touch of humor. A recent speech by the Georgia representative (a learned man "so far as I could judge, not being learned myself") had struck him blind. Feeling his fingers to see whether he was still alive, he found "a little bone left and gradually revived." The Georgian, Alfred Iverson, had charged the Whigs with abandoning Henry Clay, "like an old horse to root." But, Lincoln answered, the Democrats had done the same. Where was Martin Van Buren these days? He was supposed to get the nomination in 1844, but the Democrats rejected him on the grounds of "general availability." Whigs had no interest in that intraparty fight: "I say," concluded Lincoln about the Democrats' war against their former leader, "devil take the hindmost — and the foremost." Opponents charged Taylor supporters with hiding under the general's military coattail. But Jackson's had been long enough to cover five presidential races. "Like a horde of hungry ticks you have stuck to the tail of the Hermitage lion to the end of his life; and you are still sticking to it, and drawing loathsome sustenance from it, after he is dead."

Lincoln conceded that this might not have been the proper subject for a speech before Congress, but he wished "the gentlemen on the other side to understand, that the use of degrading figures is a game at which they may not find themselves able to take all the winnings." There were yells from the seats ("we give up, we give up") but Lincoln continued. The only military tail Cass had was the one biographers attached to him. "He invaded Canada without resistance and outvaded it without pursuit." If there was some question about whether Cass broke his sword, threw it away, or what not, it was "a fair historical compromise to say, if he did not break it, he did not do anything else with it." Cass's life reminded Lincoln of his own brief career as a military hero, of Black Hawk memory. He did not break a sword because he had none to break, but he bent a musket by accident. Not much blood was shed, except by mosquitoes; and if Cass picked huckleberries, Lincoln had raided the onion patch.

The Wilmot Proviso had stipulated that no territory acquired from Mexico should be open to slavery. On that crucial issue Cass, glimpsing "the great democratic ox gad [spear] waving in his face," went where ordered, stood still when told to, and did whatever party expediency required. And the only "charges" to which he could point were on the public treasury; as governor of Michigan territory for seventeen years he collected three different salaries, holding three separate positions at one time then acquiring three more, which brought in three further incomes.

After having examined Taylor's splendid military record Lincoln, with only three minutes left, chided his opponents for enjoying the dissent in the Whig ranks. The factions in his party were like nothing compared to those among New York Democrats — which reminded Lincoln of what the tipsy fellow once said when he heard the reading of an indictment for hog stealing. The clerk read on till he got to, and through, the words "did steal, take, and carry away, ten boars, ten sows, ten shoats, and ten pigs" at which the drunk exclaimed, "Well, by golly, that is the most equally divided gang of hogs, I ever did hear of." And the Democrats of New York were just another equally divided gang of hogs.

An active correspondence kept Lincoln in touch with Whig leaders throughout the nation. To Thaddeus Stevens he wrote for details of Whig prospects, saying, "You may possibly remember seeing me at the Philadelphia convention — introduced to you as the lone Whig star of Illinois." William Schouler, editor of the *Boston Atlas,* reported on the state of New England, and John D. McGill wrote about Virginia. But Lincoln could not help Logan, his former law partner, who ran unsuccessfully for the vacated Illinois seat against a minor war hero who let no one forget it.

Probably on behalf of Whig national headquarters Lincoln toured Massachusetts, where the Whig position was precarious. Lincoln everywhere explained that those who deserted to the Free Soilers would waste their votes, that to stop the spread of slavery it was necessary to rely on Taylor, Southerner and slave-holder though he was. Lincoln directed his argument to the Conscience Whigs; he knew that Charles Francis Adams, Charles Sumner, and John A. Andrews were not abolitionists and were subject to persuasion as also were hard-line Webster Whigs. A *Boston Daily Advertiser* reporter described the Illinois congressman as "very tall and thin . . . with an intellectual face, showing a searching mind and cool judgment." The *Atlas* respectfully reported Lincoln's address to "a glorious meeting" of the Whig club of Boston. He also spoke at rallies in Lowell, Dedham, and Cambridge, visited Taunton, and shared a platform with William H. Seward in Tremont Temple.

Mrs. Lincoln and the children joined Lincoln on the journey, by way of Springfield, Albany, Buffalo, and Niagara Falls, to Chicago, where he repeated at Old Rough and Ready rallies what he had said earlier in Massachusetts. With Illinois a doubtful state, Democratic sentiments ran high. Partisan sheets missed no chance to remind readers that the Whigs had given "aid and comfort to the enemy" or to subject Lincoln to yet another stream of abuse. He gave as good as he got. More important, his name became known throughout the nation.

In November 1848 Taylor won and, though the Democrats carried Illinois, it was by a smaller margin than four years earlier. Pleased, Lincoln prepared to pluck one of the plums sure to reward the deserving under a Whig administration. Intent on finding an appointment, he returned to Washington alone for the short session of Congress. Mary, having tasted life in the city, had had enough of it.

The slavery issue would not let him rest, though he had no desire for involvement with it. He voted with the antislavery men on the Wilmot Proviso and on California and New Mexico but against them on bondage in the District of Columbia. To mediate, Lincoln suggested a bill for gradual, compensated emancipation in Washington, provided that the district residents approved. But he dropped the idea when it drew fire from both sides. Years later Wendell Phillips made this the excuse to call Lincoln "that slave hound from Illinois." And almost at once his proposal evoked a warning and a statement of principle from John C. Calhoun. The South Carolinian warned of disaster for the South and declared that the superior white race required the enslavement of the Negro lest the section become "the abode of disorder, anarchy, poverty, misery and wretchedness."

Necessity was catching up with the Americans of his time. But Lincoln still regarded debates on this level as futile. Simpler calculations occupied him. With his district in the hands of Democrats, the time had come for the reward earned by services to his party. He had used his influence as congressman to cement support through patronage and had tried to satisfy requests for favors, appointments, offices, and commissions while balancing a variety of considerations. Walter Davis wanted a post office appointment in Springfield, and he was qualified, being a good Whig, poor, with a widowed mother to support, and not a troublemaker. But Lincoln also remembered that Davis deserted him once and had gone over to Baker. It had been possible to evade such requests while a Democrat was president. But with Taylor elected the stream of letters grew into a flood. James McLean wanted an office in Palestine, Illinois, John Bennet a place in California, Josiah B. Herrick one in Chicago, and John Murray thought himself qualified to be a marshal.

Lincoln exerted himself in vain. He wanted offices given "to gratify our friends and stimulate them to future exertions," but qualifications, personal relations, and deals counted as well, and the Taylor people trampled his wishes in the dust merely to gratify others. At the end of April 1849 he went back to Springfield disgusted. The United States judgeship for which he had pushed Logan went to someone else. Indeed not one man Lincoln had recommended was "appointed to anything, big or little, except a few who had no opposition." Places went to men who never sweated blood in the Taylor cause. The

General Land Office on which his personal hopes fixed had gone to Justin Butterfield of Chicago, a recipient of Polk handouts and a supporter of Clay. Lincoln asked several people to intercede for him and finally wrote to Taylor himself. No reply. Posts were going to yet another set of drones who never spent a dollar or lifted a finger in the fight for Taylor's election.

To make amends the administration offered Lincoln the secretaryship of the Oregon Territory, which he declined. Late in September 1849 he heard hints of the governorship of that territory. But Illinois, politically, professionally, and personally, was his home, and Oregon exile. Then, too, Mary — sensitive, often overwrought, and always worried about her own fragility — had no desire to leave the relative comforts of Springfield for the wilderness of the territory. And so it was back to the drudgery of circuit law.

Springfield had grown in size during the two years away, but little else had changed. Nor had the physical conditions improved. One of Lincoln's first cases was a suit against the city; his friend Orville H. Browning brought an action for damages after breaking a leg on an unrepaired street. Lincoln won.

Herndon had managed to keep the firm going in the old office across from the Court House. Two unwashed windows faced the yard of a store below, and seeds sprouted in the corners where dust gathered undisturbed. Here Lincoln received clients, read newspapers, told stories, and to Herndon's great annoyance, recited poetry out loud. Here he carried on a voluminous correspondence, answering many letters and losing others.

The firm's practice scarcely changed. Political prominence, for a time, attracted new clients. The Illinois Central Railroad, chartered in 1851, hired Lincoln to further its interests; and probably on its behalf he worked against the Atlantic and Mississippi Railroad. In 1853 he sought a legislative charter for a coal mining company he represented. But Lincoln took on less lobbying business than he could have. He earned some $5000 from the Illinois Central but had to sue to collect it, when the railroad decided, belatedly, that his fee was too high. After 1855 his practice became more lucrative. But he still took on three-dollar hog cases.

In March 1859, the debates with Douglas already behind him, Lincoln drafted an affidavit for Nazareth Norton, who testified that a mule whose possession was in dispute was actually his, since this particular mule "had a bad and plain scar on one of its legs." In April of that year Lincoln filed a complaint for slander, for a client who had heard the defendant say, "You swindled my family out of $300.00 and you might as well have stole it; and by God, I can prove it." And as late as January 1860 he settled a dispute over a $16.80 interest charge.

The country lawyer continued to live on Eighth Street, with a privy behind the house, and a woodpile and stable for the horse in the yard. The local blacksmith had made Lincoln a small buggy. A cow grazed in the road. No one bothered to lay out or spruce up the garden. Mary was too preoccupied with the children and herself; her husband did not care.

His manners still left a lot to be desired. The Washington polish was only skin deep. To his wife's annoyance, Lincoln loved to lie on his back in front of the fireplace, feet up, reading his newspaper. He answered the front door without the dignity of coat or shoes. Frequently but one suspender kept his trousers moored, and a pair of worn-out carpet slippers protected his feet. He favored a rarely brushed swallowtail coat, boots occasionally greased, in bad weather a blue cloak that lasted him ten years, and a tall brown hat crammed with papers and letters.

Sometimes he took the children to the office, driving Herndon to fury since the boys scurried around oblivious to all rules of behavior. The proud father adored his sons, denied them nothing, and was as blind and deaf to their faults as their mother. Neither parent ever applied the rod of discipline, and both worried about the boys' health. The slightly hysterical Mary suffered mortal terrors lest they kill themselves; and Lincoln often woke from dreadful nightmares about the fate of the "little rascals."

Mary's temper did not mellow with age. Neighbors, in time, adjusted to her loud, shrill voice, hysterical outbursts, and imagined fears. At the fierce explosions of anger everyone scurried for shelter. One after another, servants who resented her hectoring and felt exploited left; only those whom Lincoln secretly paid extra stayed. Mary indiscriminately scolded everyone around her, the children excepted, and on the slightest provocation flew into a fury, though once quieting down she tried to make amends.

In spite of his tolerance and the bonds between them, Lincoln sometimes found it difficult to be with her. On occasion he spent the night at a friend's house and sometimes brought his breakfast to the office, in order not to be home in the morning. He also enjoyed the circuit immensely. Despite his genuine devotion and love for his wife he was the only lawyer who traveled regularly to all the meetings of the courts. His frequent absences exasperated Mary, who hated to be alone in the house. Thunderstorms terrified her; when he was in town Lincoln hurried home from the office to comfort her.

Dinner guests came only rarely; neither Herndon nor Davis, one of Lincoln's most intimate friends, ever received invitations. There were several larger parties but not much socializing, perhaps another reason that drove Lincoln, who loved banter, conversation, and storytelling, to spend free evenings in local grocery stores, places Mary did not consider proper for a gentleman. Tradesmen indeed found it hard to deal with her; she ordered item after item only to return them as unsatisfactory. There was much economizing, usually on food, for when it came to clothes for herself or the children, Mary never pinched pennies. Anyone invited to the house had to admire the boys, willingly or unwillingly. Mary never tired of extolling their real or imaginary accomplishments and showing off their talents.

Uneventful, unexceptional — the domestic life of a man and a woman and their children followed its familiar course, until Necessity intruded into personal, then national, affairs.

Comfortably settled within his safe, commonplace home, A. Lincoln three times within a few years heard death knock at the door.

In December 1849 Eddie, always a weak and ailing child, sickened. His condition deteriorated despite the treatments doctors prescribed. For two months his parents anxiously watched and helplessly nursed the boy through fits and spells. He died on February 1, 1850.

Robert, then six, later remembered his mother's uncontrolled weeping, his father's haggard face, and the house in mourning. Mary sank into a depression, closed herself in her room, and refused food until her husband persuaded her to eat. At last the family left for a brief vacation in Kentucky, where Lincoln's legal services were useful in settling the estate of Mary's grandmother.

Mary, slowly recovering from the shock of Eddie's death, found comfort in religion. "Little Eddie," a poem printed by request in the *Illinois Journal* ended

> Bright is the home to him now given
> For of such is the kingdom of Heaven.

And Dr. James Smith, pastor of the First Presbyterian Church, assured her that her darling boy was indeed in heaven. Lincoln, grateful, rented a pew for her worship but resolutely refused to join the church. Nor was heaven his personal answer to the riddle of Necessity.

Hon. A. Lincoln could not long indulge in silent brooding. Zachary Taylor's death in July forced him to pronounce a eulogy in Chicago, for the party leaders by then knew his ability to fit words to listeners' emotions. After the conventional review of the president's humble beginnings, glorious military career, and short stay in the White House ("no bed of roses"), after the reminder that settlement of "the one great question of the day" (slavery in the territories) had become more difficult, after the assurance that trust in the "wisdom and beneficence" of the Maker would stave off despair — there still was something to say. The occasion forced the eulogist to ponder the inescapable Necessity: all must die. That somber thought led to a peroration quoted from his favorite poem, "Mortality," by William Knox:

> 'Tis the wink of an eye, 'tis the draught of a breath,
> From the blossoms of health to the paleness of death,
> From the gilded saloon, to the bier and the shroud, —
> Oh, why should the spirit of mortal be proud?

Lincoln may have noted, as he read on, the verses on generations:

> For we are the same our fathers have been:
> We see the same sights our fathers have seen, —
> We drink the same streams and see the same sun
> And run the same course our fathers have run.

> *They* loved; but the story *we* cannot unfold;
> They scorned, but the heart of the haughty is cold;
> They grieved, but no wail from their slumbers will come,
> They joyed, but the tongue of their gladness is dumb.

> They died! Aye, they died; we things that are now;
> That work on the turf that lies on their brow,
> And make in their dwellings a transient abode,
> Meet the things that they met on their pilgrimage road.

Thomas Lincoln had some months yet to live, although his son Abraham rarely wrote to the family. None had appeared at his wedding. From time to time he helped them out with small sums, but he made no effort to heal the strain left by his abrupt departure from home. Thomas had floundered all his life, never rising far above poverty, frequently asking for aid. Lincoln's stepbrother, John D. Johnston, equally improvident, married and a father, never could make ends meet and periodically also requested a sum that would, once and for all, set him on the road to prosperity.

While in Washington, Congressman Lincoln had received a half-illiterate letter from Johnston: Thomas would lose his land unless he paid a twenty-dollar judgment. Abraham cheerfully sent on the twenty dollars but clearly implied that the story was a fairy tale. For Johnston there was no cash but advice: Get a job. Lincoln would match every dollar earned with one of his own.

The exchange had been a reminder of a feckless life escaped by hard work, talent, and luck. Abraham had decisively rejected all invitations to come visit the folks; he had no wish to relive that painful past. He did not answer the two letters at the end of 1850. "It appeared to me I could write nothing which would do any good" he finally replied on January 12, 1851, when he heard from Harriet Hanks that his father was dying. Mary's illnesses prevented his coming. He hoped his father would recover, but "if we could meet now, it is doubtful whether it would not be more painful than pleasant." Let Thomas call on the Maker and "if it be his lot to go now," he would join "many loved ones gone before." Five days later the old man died. Lincoln did not attend the funeral. At that snip of the past, he knew that he belonged in Springfield, of Necessity.

At just about the same time, in Concord, the philosopher took as a subject what "we popularly call FATE." Emerson explained that "[each] man's power is hooped in by a necessity, which, by many experiments he touches on every side, until he learns its arc." But in the placid eastern setting, beautiful Necessity assumed a benevolent guise, guaranteeing the unity and coherence of all events, and making man "brave in believing that he cannot shun a danger that is appointed, nor incur one that is not." Beautiful Necessity assured the pure in heart that there were no contingencies, that law ruled throughout existence, although it disdained words and passed understanding.

Lincoln, who started with quite another view of Nature, could never apply the adjective "beautiful" to Necessity. Brooding over Necessity's personal meaning, he now had to give more thought than he wished to slavery, the inescapable malignancy implanted in the Republic.

He truly intended to apply himself strictly to business; frequent absences and residual chores from Washington had played havoc with the firm, and he knew he was not quite "an accomplished lawyer." In June 1850 he refused to allow friends to organize a grassroots movement to get him another term in Congress. He maintained some political connections as a member of the Illinois Whig National Committee. He disdained another chance at the Land Office but willingly supported the claims of loyal Whigs to appointments. Lincoln also participated in welcoming meetings for Louis Kossuth, champion of Hungarian liberty, who spoke of democracy as the spirit of the age: "All for the people, and all by the people."

Lincoln was not, however, among the eighty-three prominent citizens of Springfield — Whigs and Democrats — who signed a statement in support of the compromise engineered in 1850 by Henry Clay and Daniel Webster. To save the Union and settle the slavery issue, a bundle of laws admitted California as a free state and adjusted the Texas boundary. Stringent provisions for the return of fugitive slaves offset a measure banning the trade in the District of Columbia. The local newspapers and mass meetings approved of the arrangements, which imposed no duty inconsistent with the Constitution.

Lincoln was silent, not sure. On the issue of slavery in the territories newly acquired from Mexico the compromise was deliberately obscure. At some future time, when ready for statehood, the people would themselves decide whether to apply as free or slave states. But that decision would depend on whether, in the interim, settlers could arrive with and hold bondsmen. The answer to that question the compromise left to the courts.

Yet that was the nub of the matter. In the debates Senator Foote of Mississippi had pointed out that the treaty with Mexico carried the Constitution and all its guarantees into these areas. He argued, therefore, that every Southern slaveholder had the right to enter with his property and to enjoy the same free from all molestation, with the right of appeal to the judiciary from any interference by the territorial legislature. As against that frightening prospect Whigs like Lincoln had only the claim in Daniel Webster's March 7, 1850 speech that there was not at the moment within the United States a single foot of land, the character of which, in regard to its being free or slave was not fixed by some irrepealable law. That claim rested on assumptions of frightening fragility: That there would be no further additions to the nation's territory; that New Mexico would be ever uncongenial to cotton culture; and that the plantation was the only way to utilize slavery profitably. The prospect pleased only people certain of the beauty of Necessity.

Another death brought these matters to the surface of lawyer Lincoln's thoughts in June 1852. Out of respect to Henry Clay, stores closed, guns boomed, and a mourning procession formed. Lincoln pronounced the eulogy. The long address, uncertain in its thrust, made a harsh though veiled reference to abolitionists. But it also turned the great compromiser into a consistent opponent of slavery. Here Clay appeared aligned with Jefferson — committed to the Virginian's faith that "all men are created free and equal" and sensitive also to the "fire bell in the night" that warned of the threat to the Republic. The clearest statements in the eulogy criticized John C. Calhoun and other southern political eccentrics who had ridiculed the Declaration of Independence.

Perhaps because he was uncertain about slavery, perhaps because he saw little reward in campaigning, Lincoln played only a desultory role in the election of 1852. A few half-hearted speeches in Springfield and Peoria revealed the extent of his detachment. Later he recalled that until 1854 his profession (law) had almost superseded the thought of politics in his mind.

V I

A House Divided

NECESSITY RULED in the affairs of state as in those of men. As in Lincoln's life, so in the fate of his country massive forces set limits about individual action. He and his countrymen could do something, but only if they avoided extreme measures and cautiously remained within the boundaries of the possible. Intent though he was on improving his fortune through practice of the law, Lincoln as always felt politics tug at his interest. When Necessity endangered the Union, he could not stay out of public affairs; nor did he wish to, for the issues then coming to the fore absorbed an ever greater share of his life's meaning.

"Repeal of the Missouri compromise aroused him," Lincoln later said, "as he had never been before." The Northeast had heard angry attacks on the Compromise of 1850. But in central and southern Illinois, the area that defined Lincoln's life until 1854, the dominant attitude was acceptance and acquiescence. He had become yet another old-line Whig, listening to charges of treason hurled by one section against the other without actively involving himself on either side. Like Clay he truly opposed slavery in "principle and in feeling" but saw no way to eradicate it without producing "a greater evil even to the cause of human liberty itself."

But the congressional debate over Douglas's Kansas-Nebraska bill in 1854 engulfed Illinois. Territory that the Missouri Compromise of 1820 had closed to slavery now would be open to it if a majority of the settlers chose. Whether the people could also exclude slavery was unclear, for a proposal in Congress to that effect failed and, as in the Compromise of 1850, the Supreme Court retained the final voice in the matter.

Nevertheless Douglas pushed the proposed law that he justified by the doctrine of popular sovereignty. The Illinois legislature, in a special session, endorsed the measure for its faithful adherence to the principle of self-government as established by the great compromise of 1820. The act passed the United States Senate and the House by substantial majorities; and on May 30 President Pierce signed it.

During those momentous months Lincoln neither wrote nor spoke on anything even remotely connected with the storm raging across the nation. While Douglas, Salmon P. Chase, Seward, and others held audiences enthralled, Lincoln rode the circuit, continued to plead for the Illinois Central, defended a tavern keeper who wanted to sell liquor without a license, and represented a party in a divorce case. While the seizure of Anthony Burns, a fugitive slave, electrified the nation and sent Boston into mourning, Lincoln filed pleas, made motions, addressed juries, answered business correspondence, and read a novel that Mary liked. On May 30, when the Kansas-Nebraska Act became law, Lincoln, in Danville, had a busy day, trying eight cases before a jury — losing some, postponing others, and winning a few.

In the summer of 1854 Lincoln tried to straighten out his own ideas. In July he listened to Cassius Clay, the Kentucky abolitionist, who spoke outdoors because hostile officials refused him the use of the State House for a two-hour talk on the "signs of the times in our political world." Clay's exclusion from the only large building in town, the gutter journalism of the *Illinois State Register,* and Douglas's espousal of the Kansas-Nebraska bill reflected the meanness pervading the country. Congressman Lincoln lay on the ground whittling sticks.

What to do? At about that time he set down on scraps of

paper his thoughts on government and slavery. The object of government was to do for the community what the people "in their separate and individual capacities" could not do. It was the "common object of peaceful and just men" to right wrongs and to prevent murder, theft, and cheating. Such matters demanded combined action. Having expressed such unobjectionable principles, Lincoln was aware that he had said nothing apposite to the real situation.

He also privately recorded his thoughts on slavery. Every living creature defended the fruit of its labor. The volumes written by apologists to prove that slavery was a positive good persuaded no one "to take the good of it by being a slave himself." Bondage was not a matter of color, of intellectual superiority, or of interest; otherwise men with lighter skins could enslave those darker than themselves; the more intelligent could enslave the less; and any person could seize any other. None of these speculations made sense in the light of his thoughts on government. The American experiment had succeeded because it rested on affirmation of the equal rights of men. Detached from a sense of reality, vague abstractions floated away.

Reality, in the spring and summer of 1854, was the subject of tumultuous debates. Lincoln pondered the oratory in the Senate and the reports in the newspapers. The law still held his attention, but his thoughts slipped away to politics. At first he aimed only to secure the reelection of Congressman Richard Yates. But invitations to speak at rallies throughout the state forced Lincoln to explain the Nebraska issue and led him to the conclusion that Douglas and the South had departed from the ideals of the Founding Fathers and had altered the national position on slavery. The Kansas-Nebraska Act had undermined the fundamental assumption, written into the compromise of 1820, that slavery would eventually dissolve of itself. Popular sovereignty opened the territories to bondage. Only knaves and fools failed to see beneath the mask of local choice.

The campaign heated up. When Douglas refused to share a platform with him in Bloomington, Lincoln addressed a crowd of his own and labored to explicate his doctrine of Necessity. The people of the North and the South believed what they did because of circumstances; were their situations reversed, the Northerner would argue as vociferously for slavery as he now did against it. True. But the South was trying to eat the "half of the loaf of bread" reserved for freedom. The people had to restore past compromises destroyed by the slaveholding power. Lincoln would sustain the fugitive slave law (one wrong did not correct another), but he would not personally volunteer to catch any fugitives, and he hoped that those who crossed his path would run faster than he.

On October 3, 1854, the state fair opened at Springfield. The word had spread for weeks that Douglas would speak, and supporters and opponents of the Kansas-Nebraska bill poured into town, mingling with farmers exhibiting prize corn and hogs; cattle dealers out to make a fast deal; women selling jellies, breads, and jams; and a horde of politicians of every stripe. It rained heavily that day. Whoever could, jammed into the hall of the House of Representatives, and loud cheers applauded the Little Giant's "unanswerable speech" in support of the bill.

Lincoln answered the next afternoon. On that hot and muggy day he appeared in shirtsleeves, without a collar. As always, the thin and rasping tones of his voice mellowed as his self-confidence increased. The heavy Kentucky accent became less prominent. He spoke for three hours, his hair disheveled, sweat pouring down his face. Douglas listened intently then took another two hours to answer, pounding Lincoln "to pumice with his terrible war club of retort and argument" according to one side, not enough to chip at "the marble logic in it" according to others.

Lincoln delivered substantially the same speech twelve days later in Peoria. He had now hammered into coherence materials he had tried out on audiences during the past three

months. As he struggled to give form to his ideas, he discarded
the dry rhetoric of earlier times and addressed his neighbors
in the idiom familiar to them. The simple words that had displaced the high-blown language avoided vituperation or sustained abuse, expressed tolerance, understanding, and sympathy
for the South, and, for a campaign speech, were surprisingly
charitable to the opposition.

The argument was moral as well as political. Jefferson, author of the Declaration of Independence, had also formulated
the policy of excluding slavery from the territories, and all the
Founding Fathers agreed because slavery was "a monstrous injustice" and an affront to American ideals. The base principle
of self-interest on which it rested denied man's lofty character.
Blacks were human, not property. Hence the Constitution had
envisaged the end of the slave trade; and, Lincoln reminded
his audience, free Negroes nowhere received the treatment of
free horses. With reference to the "existing institution" Lincoln could not deny the "argument of necessity." The southern
people were not guilty of originating slavery, and there was no
easy way to rid them of it. Liberia could not, at once, receive
all the bondsmen, and emancipation would benefit neither
blacks nor whites. Where it had already taken hold there was
no alternative but to suffer the evil.

But the repugnant argument for the extension of human
bondage attempted to justify the introduction of slavery into
hitherto free territories. The right to self-government trum-
peted by the Kansas-Nebraska Act simply did not apply to
enslavement. "When the white man governs himself that is
self-government; but when he governs himself and also governs
another man, that is *more* than self-government — that is despotism." There were limits to local power. "God did not place
good and evil before man, telling him to make his choice. On
the contrary he did tell him there was one tree, of the fruit of
which he should not eat, upon pain of certain death." Man's
freedom, Lincoln thus argued, was conditioned on denying to
himself the forbidden fruit — of despotism.

In any case the issue was not the fate of a particular territory but of the entire Union and of its place in the world. Calhoun and the more candid supporters of slavery were at least consistent in calling the Declaration of Independence a self-evident lie. Spread of the institution deprived the American republican example of its just influence in the world and enabled the enemies of free institutions, with plausibility, to taunt the people of the United States as hypocrites. Lincoln went on to suggest that restoration of the Missouri Compromise and containment of bondage would purify the nation, so "that the succeeding millions of free happy people, the world over, shall rise up, and call us blessed, to the latest generations."

Otherwise, ominous consequences impended. In Kansas, pro-slavery and Free-Soil forces already prepared for battle. With blood once shed, the inevitable "shocks, throes and convulsions" that followed would sound "the real knell of the Union."

Speaking thus in October 1854, Lincoln had to consider seriously his own obligation to act by way of a personal political comeback. But he could not make up his mind on the appropriate course. On the one hand he passively encouraged the efforts of a group calling itself Republican to unite all Douglas opponents into a single organization. Yet when his name appeared on its state central committee without his approval, he demanded its withdrawal. He could not quiet long-felt doubts about the practical utility of third parties.

He also had another goal in view. On November 7 he won election to the state legislature as an anti-Nebraska Whig. He really wanted the seat in the United States Senate held by James Shields, running for another term with the support of Douglas and the regular Democratic party. Once elected to the legislature Lincoln resigned, having forgotten, apparently, that no member of that body could stand for the United States Senate. Since no one politically experienced could have overlooked that basic rule, the entire maneuver had probably been a ruse to test and further his senatorial aspirations. He immediately set to work gathering support, asking for voter lists and canvas results, forming new political alliances, renewing old ones.

Resourceful, experienced, and by now quite knowledgeable in the ways of Illinois politics, he zealously applied himself to the campaign. Even a cholera outbreak did not retard his efforts; for weeks, Herndon said, Lincoln slept, like Napoleon, with one eye open. Copies of the Peoria speech went far and wide, and friends from the circuit helped persuade doubtful legislators. Prudence demanded circumspection. Lincoln presented himself as a compromise Whig, did his best to avoid embarrassing associations, and candidly admitted that he had difficulty finding the path in so murky a situation.

The decision did not come until the tenth ballot, but Lincoln early became aware that he could not win. Some anti-Nebraska Democrats would under no circumstances vote for a Whig and might swing to Governor Joel Matteson, a Douglas man, who had displaced Shields. Lincoln thereupon threw his support and the election to Lyman Trumbull, an anti-Nebraska Democrat. The outcome was "still satisfactory to the general cause" if not to himself personally. No, he wrote soon after, he was not a senator, but the width of his support and the defeat of Matteson were gratifying. To show his good humor and pave the way for the next contest Lincoln dined all the anti-Nebraska legislators, an occasion for good eating, good speeches, and excellent sentiments. But not everyone took defeat graciously. Logan burst into tears when he heard the results, and Davis growled that Lincoln ought to have made it. And the loser buried himself in his office, gripped by melancholia.

In the spring and summer of 1855 disarray in national parties crushed Lincoln's hopes that the Whigs with whom he had always cast his lot could become the vehicle of all anti-Nebraska forces. The Know-Nothing phenomenon revealed the fragility of existing alignments. Suddenly many former Whigs and Free-Soilers deserted previous allegiances to support anti-immigrant candidates, thus permitting the Democrats to remain a majority in Illinois. Yet Lincoln shunned the dead end of nativism. He knew that Richard Yates, branded a Know-Nothing, had lost the votes of newly arrived English immigrants, and therefore the congressional race, and he noted that, in a contest for a seat on the state Supreme Court Logan, similarly tainted, was beaten worse "than any man ever was since elections were invented." In any case Lincoln found Know-Nothing principles as abhorrent as the proslavery ones; he could not perceive how anyone sensitive to the wrongs of the Negroes could join in a league to degrade a class of white men. Yet many good Whigs whose support he valued had drifted into the Know-Nothing, or American party. In the impending reshuffle he was willing to fuse with anybody, provided the ground was "right." He told his listeners "to stand with anybody who stands right." But he could not yet dissociate himself from "that mummy of a party" to which he had always adhered.

While Lincoln bided his time, practiced law, and said and wrote little, violence in Kansas escalated. Free-Soilers and proslavery Missourians poured in; terror spread, and rival camps armed. Illegal votes cast doubt on the legitimacy of elections, but a proslavery legislature enacted proslavery legislation.

These events thoroughly depressed Lincoln, heralding as they did a general deterioration he knew not how to arrest. Gunfire on distant plains that he had never seen recalled his forebodings at the Springfield Lyceum eighteen years earlier. Savage mobs and disregard for law tested the capability of people to govern themselves. The unwillingness to honor past agreements, manifest in the repeal of the Missouri Compromise, was the immediate cause of the crisis. But in the background, he now perceived, was a deeper moving force — the failure of expectations for the peaceful extinction of slavery that had been common in Henry Clay's generation. The inability of the good and great men of the past to effect anything in favor of gradual emancipation extinguished entirely the prospect of the peaceful disappearance of slavery. Instead, the South's peculiar institution threatened to spread across the continent. Yet without the goal of emancipation, however distant in the future, American loyalty to the sacred ideal of liberty would wane, and the Fourth of July would be only an occasion for firecrackers. Reluctantly Lincoln faced the question: Could the nation continue permanently half slave and half free? He had no answer: "May God in his mercy superintend the solution."

Lincoln took almost three months to respond to an anguished letter from Joshua Speed in Kentucky, who mourned the growing distance between the old friends. There was no quarrel between them, Lincoln wrote. Both were willing to maintain slavery where it already existed, although Northerners had to "crucify their feelings" to remain loyal to the Constitution. Expansion was another matter, and he would oppose the admission of Kansas as a slave state. But on no account would he support dissolution of the Union because of it. In August 1855 he still ruefully defined himself as a Whig and in public and private continued to argue for calm, for the ballot rather than the bullet, for temporary acceptance of unjust laws rather than armed resistance.

Still indecisive, always slow to make up his mind, he sniffed dubiously at new expedients and bided his time while Joshua Giddings, Owen Lovejoy, and others worked hard for the new Republican party. The *Illinois Journal*, Whig as ever and "opposed to fanaticism and extreme views," repeatedly attacked the new movement as yet another sectional group with a single, extreme plank. At a time when people were choosing sides, becoming Democrats, Know-Nothings, Abolitionists, or Republicans, Lincoln floated around — an old Whig without a new affiliation.

Early in 1856, however, Lincoln recognized that the old party was dead beyond revival and, in his own way, explored possible new associations on his own terms. He spoke to a meeting of anti-Nebraska editors in Decatur and helped draft a moderate platform opposed only to the extension of slavery and to Know-Nothingism, the latter to placate several Germans present. A presidential election approached, and Herndon, an active Republican for more than a year, sought to goad his partner toward a more radical position. He called a meeting in Springfield of citizens who favored "the policy of Washington and Jefferson" to elect delegates to the Republican state convention. At the head of the list stood the name of Abraham Lincoln, then traveling the circuit. This time there was no protest. On May 23, 1856 the *Journal* approved, and the next day Lincoln became an official candidate.

The state convention in Bloomington brought together old Whigs like Lincoln and Browning, radicals like Owen Lovejoy, and former Democrats like John M. Palmer, men united only by their antipathies — to the national administration, to extension of slavery, and to Douglas. On the morning the meetings opened the Chicago press carried the story of the burning of Lawrence, Kansas, by "border ruffians." A rumor spread that Charles Sumner, attacked on the Senate floor, was dying. The *Charleston Mercury* continued to argue for secession. Excitement mounted when former governor Reeder of Kansas appeared before the delegates to arouse Free-Soil sentiment.

Lincoln's "Lost Speech," reputedly the most rousing of his political career, aimed to quiet the flaming extremists and to tone down the proceedings in order to keep the old Whigs in line. His former associates held the balance of power in his estimation, and most of them, "fresh from Kentucky," refused to associate with abolitionists. He appeared on the new party's slate of national convention delegates, which consisted of Whigs and former Know-Nothings, but of no Republicans. The name Republican in fact appeared nowhere, Douglas having made it odious by his attacks.

Back in Springfield Lincoln found pretty much what he expected. Not all Whigs were ready to bury their old party. John Todd Stuart and others argued that fusion accomplished nothing save the destruction of Whiggery, and all to the advantage of the Democrats and their candidate, Buchanan. But to Lyman Trumbull Lincoln expressed hopes of holding "a good many Whigs, of conservative feelings and slight pro-slavery proclivities" by uniting the anti-Nebraska forces behind a moderate. The nomination of Chase, Seward, or Frémont by the new party would drive Stuart and his kind into Buchanan's arms. To ignore the old Whigs would be fatal. Lincoln's choice was John McLean, former Whig and justice of the Supreme Court, indubitably anti-Nebraska, who had stated categorically that Congress had the power to forbid slavery in the territories.

However, the antislavery crowd dominated what the *New York Times* called the "People's Convention" in Philadelphia. The presidential nomination went to John C. Frémont. For balance the new party needed a McLean-type moderate as his running mate, and William B. Archer, a conservative Whig, proposed Lincoln. Senator William L. Dayton of New Jersey became Frémont's vice-presidential candidate, but 110 delegates expressed their preference for Lincoln. The obscure one-term congressman from a minor state had achieved unexpected national prominence.

Although invited to speak in neighboring states, Lincoln refused to leave Illinois, where large crowds greeted him. In Princeton more than 10,000 came, and at the Alton state fair, more than 20,000. In Jacksonville a procession stretched a mile and a quarter long. Drawn by more than the festive quality of the occasion, conscious of the challenge to all political loyalties, these people were making judgments that would determine the course of their own lives and the future of the Republic.

On the stump Lincoln responded to the earnest listeners before him. In the speeches of the long campaign he hammered at the issues, referring less to Frémont's qualifications than to Buchanan's lack of them. Lincoln ignored the reign of terror in Kansas. He knew that blaming wholesale robbery, burning, rape, and murder on the aggressive, militant slave power changed few votes. Himself branded by Democratic newspapers the "high priest of abolitionism" and "the depot master of the underground railroad," he left fiery accusations to Sumner's *Crime against Kansas* and the Northern press and talked instead of history, of Douglas, of the Missouri Compromise, of the extension of slavery, and of the need for Union.

To some old Whigs who endorsed Millard Fillmore, the American party candidate, the election had only one issue — preservation of the Union at any cost. John Todd Stuart and others feared that black republicanism would array north against south and turned to Fillmore as the national alternative. A vote for Fillmore in Illinois was a vote for Buchanan, Lincoln charged. Lithographs of a confidential letter to old associates explained that Democrats wanted nothing more than division in the Free-Soil ranks, for a Frémont defeat would throw the state's electoral votes to Buchanan. Only the Republican candidate could sustain old Whig principles.

Over and over again Lincoln tried to shake off the "bear hug of disunion," the charge that the Republicans wished to divide the Union. It was not their fault that all Frémont's votes would come from the free states. Buchanan would get all of his from the slave states. The concentration of Republican strength in the North was an expected necessity but not an avowed purpose. Lincoln assured his audiences, "The Union won't be dissolved, We don't want to dissolve it." Only the opposition threatened disunity as a means of having its own way. "We won't dissolve the Union and you shan't." Somehow the speaker had identified the concept of Union with the very essence of the nation's republican institutions.

But Union, the set of arrangements that enabled the diverse peoples to govern themselves, had also become entangled with the future of slavery. The "naked and whole issue of it," said Lincoln, quoting from Webster's reply to Hayne, was "shall slavery be extended into U.S. territories now legally Free?" Frémont said, "It shall not," and Lincoln agreed.

Visions of the future provided a platform also for an appeal to working people. Free labor versus slave power became a Republican slogan. In party processions a wagon bore starving toilers displaying a banner — "Buchanan workshop ten cents a day." On the basis of George Fitzhugh's argument that slavery was a natural and necessary condition of all labor regardless of color, the *Illinois Journal* charged that "the laws of the slave states justify the holding of white men in bondage." An editorial described the "sneering contempt for free laborers" of Southern aristocrats. From a small Alabama newspaper Lincoln cut out a paragraph that defined free society as "a conglomeration of greasy mechanics, filthy operatives, small fisted farmers and moon struck theorists."

The election went much as Lincoln predicted. Buchanan won by a small margin and carried Illinois. But the Republicans took the governorship and elected four out of nine congressmen. Buchanan won because many old Whigs preferred him or Fillmore to Frémont. Among the unpersuaded was Mary Todd Lincoln. "My weak woman's heart was too Southern in feeling," she wrote her sister, "to sympathize with any but Fillmore," of whose stand on foreigners she approved; he at least would keep them "within bounds."

President Pierce's message to Congress on December 2, 1856, interpreted the election as a repudiation of Republican sectionalism. The trouble in Kansas stemmed from outside agitators. Buchanan's victory proved that people supported the inviolable rights of the sections. And, Pierce added, the Missouri Compromise had in any case been unconstitutional from the start, only acquiesced in by the South despite continuous indirect aggression from the North.

Eight days later the Illinois Republicans celebrated their achievements at a banquet in a gaily decorated hall in Chicago — plenty of food and drink, a glee club, and a band. Lincoln delivered a rebuttal of Pierce, that "rejected lover making merry at the wedding of his rival." Buchanan had succeeded only because of the split in the Free-Soil vote. The Republicans sought neither to weaken the Constitution nor to end bondage in the South. But a central idea, the equality of men, governed the United States. In the past Americans had put up

with existing inequalities but had also insisted on steady movement toward practical equality. The majority would refuse to
endorse the idea that "slavery is right in the abstract." The
future battle for a free society would cast aside Pierce's assertion that "all states as states are equal" and would support
the idea that all men are created equal.

By 1858, when Lincoln fought Douglas for the seat in the
United States Senate, the Missouri Compromise was dead and
buried beyond hope of resurrection. The Supreme Court had
destroyed any possibility for drawing a line between slave and
free territory. It thereby raised the issue of the future character
of the whole Republic.

Lincoln, though approaching the age of fifty and immersed
in an increasingly lucrative practice, could not stand apart.
All those concerns about freedom, Union, and equality that
had troubled him since 1854 now came to a head.

In 1856, when Lincoln had learned that the Court would
pass on the constitutionality of the Missouri Compromise in
the *Dred Scott* case, he had said that Republicans would abide
by the law of the land and had challenged the Democrats to
do the same. That position changed in the early spring of 1857
with rumors of a "political judgment." Worried, Lincoln jotted
down a few disjointed notes. Probably the Supreme Court
would hold Dred Scott a slave, despite his claim to freedom
by residence in territory the Missouri Compromise made free.
The Court would reach that conclusion by declaring unconstitutional any restrictions on slavery in the territories. All
would have to obey its decision. Should the Court find Scott
a slave, "the whole community must decide . . . that all persons
in like condition are rightfully slaves."

The actual decision outdid Lincoln's worst fears. Chief Justice Taney not only ruled the Missouri Compromise unconstitutional but also stated that Negroes had never been entitled
to citizenship or equality, because the Founding Fathers considered them so inferior as to enjoy no rights whites had to

respect. Jubilantly President Buchanan boasted that the nation's highest judicial tribunal had affirmed "that slavery exists in Kansas by virtue of the Constitution of the United States. Kansas is therefore as much a slave state as Georgia or South Carolina." The essence of the decision, as Lincoln read it, was that the Constitution expressly affirmed "the right of property in a slave." No territorial law, indeed no state law, could diminish that right. The Court thereby called into question the legitimacy of the Republican party, which stood for the containment of slavery and which without "history... pride... or... idols" had made a respectable showing because it presented the people with a choice for freedom. A sense of common danger had united Republicans, subduing old prejudices and loyalties. Now *Dred Scott* brought the danger closer.

The Supreme Court placed the position of Stephen A. Douglas in even greater jeopardy. By excluding congressional interference with slavery, *Dred Scott* also excluded interference by a territorial legislature, and thereby cut the ground out from under the popular sovereignty Douglas had espoused; and it had done so on the eve of his own campaign for reelection.

When Douglas spoke in Springfield in June 1857, Lincoln was present, his ambiguous feelings about the Little Giant reawakened. Lincoln remembered meeting him in Vandalia many years earlier, both men then young and ambitious — "I perhaps quite as much as he." Lincoln reflected that for himself "the race of ambition" had been "a flat failure"; for Douglas, "a splendid success." His "name fills the nation." But, he asked himself, how many remembered the name of Abraham Lincoln?

Douglas, the foremost leader of the Democratic party, a prospective president, had come to vindicate his principle of popular sovereignty. Kansas was quiet, he pointed out; if Free-Soilers refused to participate in the constitutional convention there, they had only themselves to blame for being left out. Utah was a different problem, however; the Mormons there defied the United States. Congress should abolish Utah's territorial government and place the area under martial law, for popular sovereignty did not apply to outlaws.

Dred Scott evoked the Little Giant's utmost ingenuity. The Constitution, the highest law of the land, expressed the will of the people. Any resistance to the decision would deal a blow to republican government. But, Douglas said, *Dred Scott* vindicated his Kansas-Nebraska Act and popular sovereignty. True, neither Congress nor a legislature could declare a territory free, but slavery as an institution could exist only if it had the positive support of law, and if people wished not to provide that support they need not do so. Furthermore, he went on, Republicans misinterpreted the Declaration of Independence, the signers of which had only white men in mind. Consistency would lead the Republicans to abolish all laws segregating the races, and amalgamation always lowered the level of the superior breed.

Two weeks later Lincoln spoke in the same hall. Although he charged that Douglas was a Catiline, jumping at the crack of the slave power whip in eagerness for the presidency, he spoke unemotionally, thoughtfully, simply, for he wished to keep the debate on a political, not personal level, and came with an armload of books to rebut his opponent's arguments.

Popular sovereignty at bottom was "a mere deceitful pretence for the benefit of slavery." Utah, Lincoln explained, exposed the hollowness of the concept. Douglas's doctrine entitled the Mormons in Utah to polygamy. The federal Constitution did not forbid it, and the people there peacefully approved it. Yet Douglas wished to deprive them of territorial status. By contrast, the election held in Kansas since Douglas's speech was "the most exquisite farce ever enacted." And Taney's decision in the *Dred Scott* case, though binding, lacked authority, falsified history, denied "legal public expectations," and thus was exposed to opposition. The Court had reversed itself before; the people could induce it to do so again. Lincoln read Jackson's congressional message in denial of Marshall's opinion in *McCulloch* v. *Maryland*. Although in that case the Supreme

Court had declared a national bank constitutional, the president had disagreed and had vetoed a bill to recharter it. An independent understanding of the Constitution had to guide each department in the government, indeed each individual, and not only the judges.

Finally Lincoln assailed Douglas's "counterfeit logic." Republicans who resisted slavery did not advocate the mixing of the races: "Just because I do not want a black woman for a slave, I [do not] necessarily want her for a wife." The Founding Fathers intended all men to be equal in some respects — their inalienable rights — but unequal in others (color, size, moral development, and social capacity). As to racial mixing, it flourished mostly in the South, not where blacks were free. Colonization and segregation were the answers to the race problem in the United States. In these suggestions Lincoln was consistent, both out of conviction and as a means of making emancipation palatable to his antiblack Free-Soil followers. Reprints of the speech circulated nationwide.

Depression and fighting in Kansas doomed President Buchanan's hopes for a quiet administration. Toward the end of 1857 Herndon, now Illinois bank commissioner, noted a downward trend in the economy. Banks, North and South, suspended payments, paralyzing industry. Farmers could not dispose of their crops. Unemployment spread. New York newspapers reported dangerous agitation and semistarvation in the city. The panic affected the party in office adversely and gave Republicans a new issue: the protective tariff would prevent financial panics, protect American manufacturers and laborers, and keep money at home.

Meanwhile renewed troubles in Kansas split the Democratic ranks. The Republicans denounced the constitution written in Lecompton, the territorial capital, by men elected almost entirely by proslavery voters. The people received the right to decide on only a single clause — whether to permit slavery or not. The rest of the constitution, including a clause that guaranteed the property rights of slaveholders already in Kansas, would go into effect without popular approval.

Douglas broke with Buchanan on that issue. Popular sovereignty lost all meaning if the people could not vote on the proposed state constitution. The president, however, feared a recurrence of the bloody strife. Sick of the Kansas question, he wanted only to settle the matter once and for all and was aware that resolutions by southern legislatures threatened secession should the North upset the Lecompton solution.

Sharp division within the Illinois Democratic party would not heal. The administration forces prepared to go to any length to punish the traitor; but Douglas men controlled the state convention in April 1858 and a platform adopted to thunderous applause did not even mention Buchanan. The administration hard-liners bolted to their own convention of "the national Democracy."

Some Republicans stood by and cheered; Herndon thus wrote gleeful letters to Theodore Parker and to other friends and acquaintances in the East, predicting that the administration would crush Douglas. With the two democracies at each other's throats, the Republicans were sure to win.

But the praise eastern Republican papers showered on Douglas was dangerous. The *New York Tribune* had great influence in Illinois, and Greeley's enthusiasm for Douglas's stand might cost the state organization dearly.

There were rumors that Douglas would become a Republican, utterly untrue but nonetheless disconcerting, as Herndon reported from his travels in the East. Herndon sounded out Seward but could not budge Greeley, who urged the Illinoians to forget the past and sustain the righteous — Douglas, at the moment. Governor Bissell of Illinois feared the effects on the Republicans of the growing number now enamored of Douglas, and Jesse K. Dubois plaintively asked, "Are our friends crazy?"

If the Republicans did poorly, Lincoln knew, it would be

their own fault. Prominent old Whigs like his friend Judge T. Lyle Dickey considered the Republicans too close to the abolitionists and might find a moderate anti-Lecompton refuge in the Douglas camp. Lincoln noted that few old Whigs participated in the Republican county conventions and understood that many would readily slip over to the Douglas camp.

That development threatened to frustrate Lincoln's personal ambitions, to undermine the future of the Republican party, and to obscure the choices before the country. The issue in 1858 was not Kansas, but slavery. Douglas opposed Lecompton because it failed not by the test of freedom but by that of popular sovereignty. The Republicans alone condemned slavery as a moral wrong, to be tolerated where it was for the moment, but to be set on the course of ultimate extinction. And *Dred Scott* made it more important than ever to present that issue to the American people.

Hence Lincoln responded when party sentiment crystalized around him as the senatorial nominee. The editor of the *Chicago Press and Tribune* had no doubt: To save the Illinois party Lincoln had to run again.

A long campaign solicited support from local politicians and attempted to halt the drift to Douglas. Lincoln refused to credit rumors of "secret arrangements" by which Greeley and Seward would support Douglas in return for an endorsement of Seward for the presidency in 1860. Greeley, erratic as he was, was also a man of principle. Lincoln therefore abstained from any retaliatory action and hastened to assure Charles L. Wilson that the Republicans of Illinois were entering into no secret arrangements: "Neither I, nor any friend so far as I know, has been setting [a] stake against Governor Seward [of New York]." But careful negotiation by his cronies ensured a successful outcome at the party convention in Springfield.

Republicans thronged into the state capital for the convention on a lovely springlike day, June 16, 1858, hopeful, their chances never before as good. Harmony made a careful check of credentials unnecessary. All comers were welcome. In recognition of the German vote Gustave Koerner was made president of the assembly. A platform written under the direction of Orville H. Browning upheld states' rights — where slavery existed it would be left alone. The party approved proposals for a homestead law, affirmed the rights of free labor, and condemned the *Dred Scott* decision. Congress had power to keep bondage out of the territories, and "no power on earth" could "maintain slavery in the States against the will of their people." The United States was not to enter into any entangling alliances, and injuries to Americans on high seas had to be redressed. An unprecedented declaration in the platform also announced that Abraham Lincoln was the Republican candidate for senator.

Lincoln knew of the scheme to avoid a floor contest by prejudging the issue in the platform and made sure it remained under wraps. He had instructed campaign workers not to push expressions of preference for his senatorial candidacy at county or other local conventions and meetings. "When the Republicans of the whole state get together at the State Convention the thing will then be thought of and something will or will not be done, according as the united judgment may dictate." Nevertheless several local conventions passed resolutions for Lincoln. Now the Chicago delegation brought in a banner "Cook county is for Abraham Lincoln." The crowds cheered. A Peoria delegate moved a change in the motto to "Illinois is for Abraham Lincoln," and Charles L. Wilson submitted the resolution nominating Lincoln to be the Republican candidate for the Senate from Illinois. Banners announcing "Every man for Lincoln" unfurled, and the nomination sailed through.

The day before the convention met, a letter to Greeley compared the prospective candidate favorably with Douglas. His manner on the stump was particularly attractive. "Lincoln is colloquial, affable, good natured, almost jolly. He states the case at issue with so much easy good humor and fairness that his opponents are almost persuaded he is not an opponent at all." Lincoln in the Senate would be the right man in the right place.

Conscious of the importance of the occasion, Lincoln had taken great pains with his next speech. For weeks he had prepared the arguments against Douglas, jotting down notes on envelopes and bits of paper, which he stored in his hat. When he had written the talk out he read the lines to Dubois and Herndon, then rehearsed it with others in the State Library.

But though carefully prepared, the speech did not groan under the weight of formal rhetoric as his earlier orations had. Short, studded with memorable phrases, it avoided high-blown language. Simple sentences, brief paragraphs, and carefully chosen, plainly presented examples expressed clear thoughts without ambiguities. Lincoln by 1858 had learned to adapt to a contrived address the informal style of his impromptu conversation. He reduced complex issues, such as squatter sovereignty and the *Dred Scott* case, to bare bones, starkly presented.

Before a crowded hall of representatives, Lincoln delivered his address on June 16, 1858. He read slowly from a manuscript, emphasizing words he had underlined in the text; and he made sure that the italics stayed in print when the speech appeared in the *Illinois Journal*. The larger Republican newspapers in Illinois reprinted it in its entirety; smaller ones ran long excerpts. It also became a campaign document, circulated by the Republican State Committee. It pleased Theodore Parker, to whom Herndon promptly forwarded a copy, and also Greeley, whose *New York Tribune* gave readers the full text. Talk that Illinois Republicans might vote for Douglas ended.

Aware that errant Republicans and unattached old Whigs might stray into the Douglas fold, Lincoln insisted that support for his opponent, even on a single issue, would lead to total triumph of the Democratic party. On the Lecompton constitution, Douglas agreed with the Republicans. But he had not changed his views on other matters. He still upheld popular sovereignty and devoted his efforts to clearing the ring and giving slavery and freedom a fair fight. He had openly declared that he did not care whether slavery was voted up or down. But self-government, the Republicans believed, was not the issue. To hold people in bondage was not a matter of self-government. There could be no fair fight between slavery and freedom, for one was morally wrong, the other morally right. Douglas, however, was consistent; having all along insisted that slavery was as good as freedom, he had sought to bring the people of the nation to not care anything about slavery. But Republicans knew that slavery was a deadly poison. In the past the nation had acquiesced out of "necessity" in the South's peculiar institution but had not thereby mortgaged the future.

Now the Nebraska doctrine, the *Dred Scott* decision, the principle of squatter sovereignty, and the actions of the Buchanan administration, all cogs of a single "piece of machinery," revealed a design tending to the idea that "if any one man chooses to enslave another, no third man shall be allowed to object." One could not know absolutely that all these pieces of machinery were the result of a preconcert. But when different workmen, named Stephen, Franklin, Roger, and James, at different times and places succeeded in fitting together a perfect wooden frame, this was evidence of a common plan or draft. And, unless overthrown, the power of the present political dynasty would spread slavery under the guise of another Supreme Court decision declaring that the Constitution of the United States prohibited a state from excluding bondage from within its boundaries. Caged and toothless, Douglas was not the lion to prevent that outcome. He did not care about the advance of slavery. The Republicans alone did.

"A house divided against itself cannot stand." Almost a year before at Springfield, Lincoln had backed away from that sentence recalled from the Scriptures. Now in June 1858 it was clear: The issue was not Kansas or the territories, but the limitless extension of slavery everywhere and into the future. Therefore "the government cannot endure permanently half slave and half free." He did not expect the Union to dissolve or the house to fall, but he did expect it to cease to be divided, becoming either completely slave or completely free. The *Dred Scott* decision had opened the door. Little even now remained to be done to gratify the slaveholders. With "the deceitful cloak of self government" swept away and the "intervening trash [and] compacts" eliminated, the battle lines were drawn in the struggle between those who cared for the liquidation of slavery and those who fought against it.

Douglas and the Democrats believed that a house divided could indeed stand, with some chambers free and others not. The Union for them was the product of the Constitution, a compact among sovereign states. But the more Lincoln learned of the past, and particularly since the *Dred Scott* decision forced him to read the views of the Founding Fathers, the more convinced he became that the nation was the product not of the Constitution (which only formed a *more perfect* Union) but of the Declaration of Independence. A few months earlier, explaining the importance of Fourth of July celebrations to a Chicago audience, he had noted that immigrants could find no connection by blood to the glorious epoch of the Revolution. "But when they look through that old Declaration of Independence they find that those old men say that 'We hold these truths to be self-evident, that all men are created equal,' and then they feel that that moral sentiment taught in that day evidences their relation to those men, that it is the father of all moral principle in them, and that they have a right to claim it as though they were blood of the blood and flesh of the flesh of the men who wrote that Declaration, and so they are. That is the electric cord in that Declaration that links the hearts of patriotic and liberty-loving men together, that will link those patriotic hearts as long as the love of freedom exists in the minds of men throughout the world."

In the months that followed the nomination Lincoln would explore the implications of a Union that sprang from the commitment to freedom in the Declaration of Independence. But already he knew that, at the very least, such a house could not stand, half-slave, half-free.

What would come to pass, Lincoln did not say. He clearly preferred peaceful ballots to bloody bullets. A choice was possible: "It only needs that every right thinking man shall go to the polls and without fear or prejudice, vote as he thinks."

VII

Disunion

THE SENATORIAL CANDIDATES, moving about by rail, could not fail to perceive the state's transformation. Year by year the transportation network had grown. The Illinois and Michigan Canal had linked the Great Lakes and the Mississippi in 1848, the same year in which the telegram reached Chicago. Ten years later eleven main railroad lines ran into that city, the population of which soared from 29,000 to 112,000 between 1850 and 1860. In the same decade the number of people in Illinois swelled from 851,000 to 1,711,000. Concealed in those figures was a change in the character of the state's residents. The percentage of northern origin remained constant; but the percentage of southerners declined, their places filled by foreign immigrants. As a result, the internal political balance tilted toward voters unsympathetic to slavery.

The consequences of the contest for the senatorial seat rippled out beyond the borders of Illinois and profoundly influenced the presidential election of 1860 and the momentous events that followed. In that broader context the result of the Senate race was less important than the running debate that preceded the balloting. For the first time correspondents traveled with the candidates, taking down speeches stenographically. Eagerly attended, carried by telegraph, and promptly reprinted or reported in the eastern press, the discussions attracted nationwide interest. The striking contrast between the two central characters converted these encounters into dramatic contests. Listeners and readers intently followed the clash of rivals who had sprung from similar backgrounds and now occupied opposing grounds. But more than that accounted for the concern with which Americans followed the accounts from remote Illinois towns. What the debaters said in Freeport or Jonesboro had meaning in Boston and Richmond because the flow of words plainly exposed the destined dilemma from which the nation would not escape.

In the "House Divided" speech, Lincoln threw down the gauntlet. Douglas responded. Exposed to frontal attacks by the Republicans, he also had to deal at his rear with Buchanan Democrats who picked off officeholders loyal to him. His enemies he knew were not above some measure of cooperation to ensure his defeat.

Douglas returned from Washington to a triumphal welcome in Chicago; and more than 10,000 people came to hear him speak from a hotel balcony. Lincoln had arrived from Springfield the night before and listened closely, taking notes, observing his opponent. Douglas referred to his rival as "kind, amiable, an intelligent gentleman, a good citizen and an honorable opponent" and promised that the issues between them would be those of principle and not personality. That element of courtesy would not long endure.

When Douglas finished, the crowd shouted for more. At the corner of Lake and Dearborn streets fireworks revealed flaming letters that spelled out Popular Sovereignty. To shouts calling for a rejoinder Lincoln answered by pointing to the lateness of the hour. But he responded the next evening, from the same balcony. The exchange attracted national attention. Although partisan newspapers praised their favorites and judged their own crowds bigger, more enthusiastic, more intelligent, and more committed, all agreed that Lincoln and Douglas were worthy foes. The *New York Times* declared Illinois "the most interesting political battle ground in the Union."

For the next few days the candidates stayed in Chicago, arranging their campaigns. State Republican leaders warned

Lincoln against a defensive posture. He had to attack by following Douglas wherever he went.

Douglas traveled to Springfield in style, in a private railroad car, sipping brandy and smoking cigars, attended by his wife, a small secretarial staff, and many reporters. Lincoln took the same train but traveled coach. At each stop crowds gathered and bands played. In Bloomington, Republican territory, Douglas made another speech, attracting 2000 listeners in spite of the pouring rain. Lincoln listened but refused to respond. Dismal, reflective, dusty, and tired, he walked alone, carpetbag in hand, wearing his long, loosely-fitted frock coat and weather-beaten silk hat to the hotel where he spent the night. The next morning everyone resumed the journey to Springfield, where a large crowd waited despite the heavy rain. Umbrella in hand, his coat skirts flapping in the wind, Lincoln descended, jumped over a rail fence, and disappeared. Douglas did not miss the chance for yet another address.

Lincoln fretted, still on the defensive. Although an encouraging letter from Horace Greeley promised help, party managers worried. Douglas was making headway and held the old Whigs of central and southern Illinois who had refused to follow Lincoln two years before. The former Know-Nothings were also in doubt, on the verge of a stampede to the Democrats.

The list of speaking appointments published by Douglas headquarters in Springfield covered a great part of the state. In response Lincoln arranged counter meetings, some in places and at times parallel to those of Douglas, others on the following days. Democrats scoffed at an opponent who could only trail their candidate. But they worried, when, under party pressure, Lincoln proposed a series of debates. Douglas demurred; debates would only give Lincoln greater publicity. Thereupon the Republican newspapers announced that Lincoln had made the offer and that the cowardly Democrat would decline. In the end Douglas agreed, specifying places and times. What "a long winded pettifoging reply" was this, the Republican press sneered: "the little dodger," afraid of "Long Abe," shirked and backed out except for seven places he himself selected.

On August 21, 1858, the candidates met in Ottawa for the first debate. On this hot and sunny day wagons filled with farm families crowded the town. Other people came on horseback, and many walked. Banners, flags, and signs sprouted everywhere, cannons roared, bands played, and peddlers hawked Lincoln or Douglas badges. Rival processions greeted their favorites, as mounted marshals and aides vainly tried to maintain order. Lincoln arrived on a special train, escorted by fourteen cars of shouting Republicans. Douglas came from Peru in a grand carriage drawn by four splendid horses; hundreds of mounted followers accompanied him into town, making a way through the throngs with great difficulty.

The debate took place in the town square, the candidates sitting on a raised platform. Douglas looked imperiously at the assembly, tossing his hair; Lincoln seemed subdued and humble. At least 12,000 people were on hand for the opening at two in the afternoon.

On this occasion, as on three others, Douglas made the first statement (one hour), Lincoln the second (one hour and a half), and Douglas responded (a half hour). In the other three debates the candidates reversed the roles. A timekeeper ensured fairness. The format compelled the candidate to listen to his opponent's position and answer; and the unfolding dialectical argument forced each to clarify his position.

It rained in Freeport the day of the second debate. Nevertheless 15,000 people filled the area beyond capacity. Douglas walked to the platform, dressed "plantation style" — in rich attire, including a ruffled shirt, dark blue coat with shining buttons, light trousers, and a wide-brimmed soft hat. Lincoln, dusty and shabby, had just alighted from a lumbering old wagon filled with farmers, as if to emphasize his identity with the common folk. In Jonesboro, site of the third debate, the southern audience was heavily Democratic and not as large as elsewhere. By contrast the fourth encounter at Charleston on September 18 drew a crowd larger than that at Freeport, for old Whigs lived in this area. An immense banner with a painting of "Old Abe" greeted him on arrival. Emphasis was on Whig continuity:

> Westward the star of empire takes its way
> The girls link-on to Lincoln, as their
> mothers did to Clay.

October 7 saw the candidates at Galesburg in a heavy rain. A large Republican banner read: "Small-fisted farmers, mud sills of society, greasy mechanics for A. Lincoln," borrowing the phrases of South Carolina's Senator Hammond who had explained that every community required unskilled labor directed by superiors; southern slaves and northern hirelings were both "the mud sills" of society. There followed debates at Quincy (October 13) and Alton (October 15).

About the debates, widely reported as they were, spilled a turbulent tributary flow of oratory. By his own count, Lincoln made 63 speeches, Douglas 130, including impromptu responses and unscheduled addresses. This stream of words poured along several well-defined currents.

Personal attack and misrepresentation, tolerated by the rules of political combat, probably swayed few voters. The Democrats used the Aurora resolutions, which Lincoln had actually defeated, to identify him with the abolitionism he had rejected. When Republicans denounced the "forgery," Douglas wired a henchman, "The hell hounds are on my track. For God's sake, Linder, come and help me fight them." The telegraph operator sold a copy to the Republicans, who promptly published it. Democrats did not fail to charge Lincoln with lack of patriotism during the Mexican War. Newspapers reproduced a jingle popular years before:

> Mr. Speaker! Spot! Spot! Spot!
> Mr. Speaker! Where's the Spot!

Is it in Spain or is it not?
Mr. Speaker! Spot! Spot! Spot!

Lincoln's denial that he had abandoned American soldiers to
Mexican barbarity did no good; it only lent credibility to criticism of his lack of experience.

Lincoln accepted the role of underdog and capitalized on it.
He never tired of pointing out the worldwide fame of his rival,
which he contrasted with his own humble status. "I am not
[a] master of language," he too often conceded. "I have not a
fine education, I am not capable of entering into a disquisition
upon dialectics." Democrats of course looked to Douglas as the
future president, seeing in his "round, jolly, fruitful face post
offices, land offices and marshallships and cabinet appointments" as well as numerous other plums on which to lay their
greedy hands. Alas, Lincoln went on, nobody ever expected
him to be president: "In my poor, lean, lank face nobody has
ever seen that any cabbages were sprouting." Since Lincoln
was, in actuality, the better phrase maker and the more effective speaker, with a finer ear for language tones, he turned his
rival's handsome appearance into a liability, appealed for audience sympathy and solidarity, and moved to the attack,
keeping Douglas on the defensive.

The give and take of these exchanges amused audiences,
fixed attention on the performances of the Little Giant and
Old Abe, and held national interest. But beyond the banter
and the thundering charges lay a serious pursuit of the meaning of serious problems; questions raised elicited answers that
raised other questions and stimulated thought about the very
nature of the Republic.

The point of departure was popular sovereignty, with which
Douglas had associated himself since repeal of the Missouri
Compromise in 1854. Before the second debate Lincoln framed
the following inquiry: "Can the people of a United States Territory in any lawful way against the wish of any citizen of the

United States, exclude slavery from its limits prior to the formation of a State Constitution?" The *Dred Scott* decision had answered in the negative and had thereby cast doubt on the future of freedom.

Douglas had often addressed the embarrassing and divisive question. Yet to restate his position might reopen the quarrel with President Buchanan and might antagonize Southerners, who now argued that local laws could not exclude slavery from any territory. His response, aiming to please all, satisfied none. The right of the people to make a territory slave or free was "perfect and complete" because the institution could not exist anywhere unless supported by local police regulations. The people could elect an antislavery legislature that would refuse to enact the legislation essential to the survival of bondage. The response would cost Douglas dearly in the South, yet it also troubled Northerners by allowing local governments to override the Constitution as interpreted by the courts.

By the time Lincoln raised a corollary question, Douglas had readied an answer, to which Lincoln in turn responded.

Question: How could a legislature, the members of which took an oath to support the federal Constitution, pass laws unfriendly to slavery, when *Dred Scott* had affirmed the constitutional guarantee of property in slaves?

Answer: Slave property is on equal footing with other property, use of which legislatures could also regulate — liquor, for instance.

Response: Douglas "sang paeans" to popular sovereignty until the Supreme Court had "squatted his squatter sovereignty out." He had "invented this sort of do-nothing sovereignty — that the people may exclude slavery by a sort of sovereignty that is exercised by doing nothing at all. Is that not running his popular sovereignty down awfully? . . . Has it not got down as thin as the homeopathic soup that was made by boiling the shadow of a pigeon that had starved to death?" *Dred Scott* had covered the whole issue; there was "no room even for the shadow of a starved pigeon to occupy the same ground."

To dissociate himself from the firebrands in his own party, Lincoln promised to maintain slavery in the South and to support the recovery of fugitives. He would not impose freedom on the District of Columbia or attempt to abolish the internal slave trade. He was not an abolitionist. But he recognized the evil of slavery and hammered away at the moral obtuseness of his opponent who did not. "You say it must not be opposed in the free States, because slavery is not here; it must not be opposed in the slave States because it is there; it must not be opposed in politics, because that will make a fuss; it must not be opposed in the pulpit, because it is not religion. ... Then where is the place to oppose it?" "That is the real issue," Lincoln said in the final debate. "That is the issue that will continue in this country when these poor tongues of Judge Douglas and myself shall be silent. It is the eternal struggle between these two principles — right and wrong — throughout the world."

Douglas responded with a plea for pluralism. Uniformity in local laws and domestic institutions was the parent of despotism; the diversity recognized in the Constitution was the greatest safeguard of the rights of citizens. The nation could endure half-slave and half-free: it had done so until radicals and designing politicians had thrust forward irrelevant moral judgments and forebodings: "The people of the slave holding States are civilized men as well as ourselves, ... they bear consciences as well as we, and ... are accountable to God and their posterity, and not to us. It is for them to decide, therefore, the moral and religious right of the slavery question for themselves, within their own limits." It did not become anyone else to tell the people of Kentucky that they had no consciences, that they lived in a state of iniquity, and that they cherished an institution in violation of divine law. It was better to "judge not, lest ye shall be judged." Northerners could attend to enough objects of charity in the free states without going abroad in search of Negroes.

Lincoln denied, of course, that he favored a general consolidation of all the local institutions of the various States. Each state could do with such matters as it liked; Illinoians put up with Indiana's cranberry laws or Maine's liquor laws, like them or not. But bondage was not on a par with cranberries or whiskey. For a vast majority of Americans slavery was a moral evil, and "not . . . an evil merely confining itself in the States where it exists." The government of the United States had endured for decades half-slave and half-free, but only because all its people believed slavery would die out. The signers of the Declaration of Independence and authors of the Constitution certainly thought so, which was why they meant to exclude slavery from the territories. They had submitted to slavery where it already existed. But, Lincoln reminded his audience, Christ had said, "Be ye [therefore] perfect even as your Father which is in heaven is perfect," without expecting anyone to measure up to that standard. The principle of men's equality was such a standard, to be reached as nearly as men could. "If we cannot give freedom to every creature, let us do nothing that will impose slavery upon any other creature."

The Kansas-Nebraska Act, under the cloak of popular sovereignty, had breached the old understanding about the future by expanding the vistas for slavery, and *Dred Scott* had gone even further by abrogating popular sovereignty. No matter how Douglas twisted matters about, the people could not keep slaves out of a territory. The institution would take root in each new state before it adopted a constitution. And before long, filibusters would expand the boundaries of the United States to condemn ever more areas to bondage. The sequence of events suggested a plot for the sole purpose of nationalizing slavery. The evidence proved the existence of the conspiracy, and if Douglas denied all knowledge of it, that only showed that the conspirators used him without his knowledge.

Douglas rejoined that the "law of the formation of the earth, the ordinances of Nature, or the will of God" destined the West to freedom. Slavery would not flourish there and would disappear wherever it ceased to be profitable. His opponent pointed out, however, that geography was no barrier to slavery, as large parts of Kentucky, Virginia, Maryland, and Delaware reached as far north as parts of Ohio, Indiana, and Illinois. Further, the Supreme Court might some day extend the logic of *Dred Scott* to hold free states' constitutions unconstitutional.

At the very suggestion, the Little Giant fumed. "No man on the bench could ever descend to" such an act of moral treason. Thereupon Lincoln recalled that support for the first *Dred Scott* decision committed Douglas to the next, which in time would make slavery national and spread it across the Western Hemisphere.

Douglas parried these damaging thrusts on the issue of freedom with the awkward issue of race and crowded Lincoln into a corner, particularly when debating in areas settled from the South. The Little Giant argued that the government "was made by the white man for the white man to be administered by the white man." He cared more "for the great principle of self government" than "for all the negroes in Christendom." He would not endanger the Union or "blot out the great inalienable rights of the white men for all the negroes that ever existed." Each state had to determine for itself the extent to which it accorded rights to inferior peoples. Racial equality in the end meant "the right of amalgamation." All whites — German, English, American, and Irish — were equal; the blacks were not. He had seen Frederick Douglass ride into town with two white women. Perhaps the black Republicans wanted that. The "monstrous revolutionary doctrine" of racial intermingling would prevail if Lincoln won. The crowds responded, "He shall not."

Old Abe never denied the whiteness of American government; the charge of a belief in "negro equality" was "but a specious and fantastic arrangement of words, by which a man can prove a horse chesnut to be a chesnut horse." He affirmed white supremacy. Social equality was irrelevant. There were enough whites and blacks of both sexes to marry their own kind, and the races would not mix in the territories if the inferior was not allowed to go there. The exclusion of slaves would make the West an asylum where "Hans, and Baptiste, and Patrick, and all other men from all the world may find new homes and better their condition in life."

But though inferior to whites, blacks were human beings entitled to rights by the fundamental American assertion that all men were created equal. If the Declaration of Independence had meant what Douglas said it did, it should have added "except the negroes." Douglas's reasoning was of a kind with "the arguments that kings ... made for enslaving the people in all ages of the world ... the same old serpent that says, You work and I eat." All Lincoln asked for the Negro was "that if you do not like him, let him alone. If God gave him but little, that little let him enjoy." As between the white and the black, choose the white; but as between the black and the crocodile, choose the black. "As I would not be a *slave,* so I would not be a *master.* This expresses my idea of democracy."

Pressed on the issue in central Illinois, where old Whigs wavered, Lincoln went further. Never in any way had he favored the social and political equality of the races. Negroes should not be voters, jurors, or officeholders, nor should they marry whites: "I as much as any other man am in favor of having the superior position assigned to the white race." Neither he nor his friends intended to marry Negroes; and if Douglas and his supporters feared that, he would support laws to prevent it. Illinois indeed already had such a statute, and Lincoln would to the end stand by it.

Exasperated, Douglas attacked the shifty great Free-soil Abolition party, incapable of assuming one name, parading under different guises in different counties, all to cheat the people by obscuring the fact that it was but an amalgam of

Black Republicanism. "Their principles in the north are jet-black, in the center they are in color a decent mulatto and in lower Egypt they are almost white. A house divided against itself cannot stand. Well, look at the Republican party." If elected and sworn to uphold the Constitution of the United States, would Lincoln mean "the Constitution as he expounds it in Galesburg, or the Constitution as he expounds it in Charleston?"

Lincoln indignantly denied that he expressed different views in different parts of the state. Certainly he knew that every speech he made, wherever delivered, would be put into print so that all the reading and intelligent people in the community would see it and know his opinions. Still he drew an exceedingly fine line in opposition to both Negro citizenship and slavery. The effort to hold both positions trapped him as it continued to trap his countrymen for a century more. The Negro was not equal but was entitled to the rights enumerated in the Declaration of Independence. The doctrine invented by Taney in *Dred Scott* and sustained by Douglas had an evil tendency, if not an evil design. It dehumanized the Negro. "I combat it as being one of the thousand things constantly done in these days to prepare the public mind to make property, and nothing but property, of the negro in all the States of this union."

The turnout was good when Illinois voters went to the polls on a rainy November day. They elected legislators committed to one or another of the candidates. The total popular vote for those pledged to Lincoln ran ahead of that for the Douglas people: 125,430 to 121,609. But the distribution of seats in the legislature had not kept pace with changes in population, and there Douglas won, 54 to 46.

Douglas nevertheless proved the greater sufferer in the aftermath of the debates, not at once but two years later, when the house proved indeed divided against itself. The debates clarified the meaning of his stand on slavery in the territories, so that neither the South nor the North accepted it; Lincoln, however, became a national figure.

Failure to win the Senate seat disappointed but did not discourage Lincoln. As standard-bearer he had contributed to the party coffers, no matter how strained his own circumstances, so that the campaign exhausted him financially as well as physically. But the cause of civil liberty would triumph, he knew. Democratic harmony would not last long, and the Republicans would be ready to exploit another explosion soon. He had no intention of sinking out of view. Small-town Illinois newspapers suggested he would make a good presidential candidate in 1860, others that he would be a perfect running mate for Seward.

In the early weeks of 1859 he outlined the Republican strategy, urging caution, restraint, and moderation. For the sake of the cause the party had to unite and attract as broad a base of support as possible. No quibbling over fine points! To a Chicago audience on March 1, 1859, he stated the cause: slavery as a "moral, political and social wrong"; nothing "minor or subsidiary to that main principle and purpose" should intrude. The Republicans were the true heirs of Jefferson. They were for "both the man and the dollar," but in cases of conflict, "the man before the dollar," while the Democrats held "the liberty of one man to be absolutely nothing when in conflict with another man's right of property." The defenders of a free society had to be on guard. Those who would not be slaves must consent not to have others as slaves.

To occupy the middle ground that would ensure an 1860 victory the Republicans had to win over the old Whigs and prevent Douglas from leading northerners astray to the pipe of popular sovereignty. Agitation of questions like Oregon's admission as a free state or repeal of the fugitive slave law would gain no electoral vote, it would only complete the alienation of people like John Todd Stuart and James B. Clay, son of the sainted Henry.

In 1859 Douglas was again the rival for moderate support. Were he to despair of the Southern vote and risk all on the Northern following, he might absorb the Republican party in a grouping that took no forthright stand on the morality of slavery. And indeed, in 1859 he moved to occupy the moderate national position. Blaming Southern leadership for recent defeats, he determined to make himself the Democratic standard-bearer on the basis of a platform set forth in a long article in *Harper's* magazine. Popular sovereignty he treated as the cornerstone of American political thought, establishing local control over all domestic matters, slavery included. He drew a sharp dividing line between domestic affairs and the nation's general welfare; in the former sphere local authority prevailed.

Lincoln took notes on the subsequent newspaper debate, for he believed the entire argument baseless. The Founding Fathers controlled slavery in the territories and did the identical thing which Douglas insisted they understood they ought not to do.

The chief danger to the nation, said Lincoln, was "that insidious Douglas Popular Sovereignty" doctrine. Everyone could agree "that each man shall do precisely as he pleases with himself." But, in effect, Douglas maintained that "If one man chooses to make a slave of another man, neither that other man nor anybody else has a right to object." In doing so he falsified American history and misread the Constitution and the Declaration of Independence.

In the fall of 1859 the running controversy revealed another danger of popular sovereignty. Lincoln then argued more insistently that not only the Negro's fate but everyone's was at stake. Competition with slaves degraded the labor of free white men, who had a right to the territories for themselves and posterity. His own experience refuted Southern charges that

Northern workers were worse off than slaves. Twenty-five years earlier he had been a hired laborer, but such a person toiled on his own account and would "hire others to labor for him tomorrow." Advancement was the rule of a free society. Labor was the common burden of the human race, but "the great, durable curse of the race" was the effort to shift that burden onto the shoulders of others. Free labor "has the inspiration of hope, pure slavery has no hope," only the rod. Therein lay the difference. That winter, in Wisconsin, Kansas, and elsewhere, Lincoln reiterated the warning that an acquiescent attitude would ultimately enslave all laborers, white and black.

Lincoln kept his head, as few other Americans did, after John Brown's raid on Harpers Ferry. Douglas and the Democrats immediately linked the raid to the Republican party, as the inevitable result of talk about an irrepressible conflict. Worried Republicans vehemently denied the charges and privately expressed the wish: "The old idiot — the quicker they hang him and get him out of the way the better." Lincoln, while conceding the old man's madness, nevertheless added that Brown had shown great courage and rare unselfishness. Slavery, not the Republicans, fostered such outrages. The wrong did not excuse violence, bloodshed, and treason; and death was an appropriate punishment for defiance of the law. But the incident stood also as a warning to the South. "If constitutionally we elect a President and . . . you undertake to destroy the Union, it will be our duty to deal with you as old John Brown has been dealt with." The ballot box — the peaceful method provided by the constitution was the only exit from the American dilemma. "We hope and believe that in no section will a majority so act as to render such extreme measures necessary."

Lincoln was firm yet conciliatory when he spoke at Cooper Union in New York City on February 27, 1860. His party was neither radical nor revolutionary but conservative. It was sectional only because the South made it so by rejecting venerable policies. Republicans would do their share to preserve peace by avoiding any action to disturb present arrangements. But the threat of secession in the event of a Republican victory was a highwayman's pistol held to his victim's head.

The whole controversy turned about the South's peculiar institution. "All they ask, we could readily grant, if we thought slavery right. [All] we ask, they could as readily grant, if they thought it wrong. [Thinking it right], as they do, they are not to blame for desiring its full recognition, as being right, but thinking it wrong, as we do, can we yield to them?" The nation had to stand fast. "Let us have faith that right makes might and in that faith let us, to the end, dare to do our duty as we understand it."

In spite of a snowstorm 1500 people had turned out to hear him. David Dudley Field and William Cullen Bryant shared the platform. Horace Greeley noted the presence of the largest gathering of the city's intellectual and cultural figures since the days of Clay and Webster. Four New York papers printed the speech in full, and editors lavished praises on it. The *Illinois Journal* and the *New York Herald* brought it out in pamphlet form. The Springfield lawyer, his new broadcloth suit made for the occasion but rumpled by the two-day trip, had become a national figure.

Torn by self-doubt, unconvinced that he could win, Lincoln did not consider himself a candidate. Norman Judd and others did. Illinois, now the fourth largest state in the Union, would be pivotal in the Republican convention and in the election. In 1860 the South and New England would balance one another. The decision would depend on New Jersey, Pennsylvania, Ohio, Indiana, and Illinois, the lower counties of which were Southern like the border states. Frémont, Seward, and Chase were weak there. Lincoln might carry those "doubtful states." In January 1860 Judd and several cronies from the circuit formed a secret caucus to launch the candidacy.

Meanwhile Lincoln behaved in a fashion not inconsistent with availability for the race. He spoke repeatedly throughout New England, stressing the rights of free labor. In Hartford, where shoemakers were out, he approved a system under which laborers could strike when they wanted to and were not obliged to work whether paid or not. He did not believe in a law to prevent anyone from getting rich. But he did "wish to allow the humblest man an equal chance to get rich with everybody else. When one starts poor, as most do in the race of life, free society is such that he knows he can better his condition; he knows that there is no fixed condition of labor, for his whole life." Lincoln lost no chance to remind his audiences of his own humble background and rough life. Every poor man's son, black or white, deserved the opportunities for improvement he had enjoyed.

Judd's analysis proved correct. The long-time loser who had continued to lose for more than a decade now grabbed the biggest prize of all.

The national convention, meeting in Chicago in May 1860, nominated Lincoln on the third ballot. By then a national network of friends had made his availability known. He stayed out of party squabbles and appeared the ideal candidate to the opponents of everyone else. Seward and Chase were too extreme for some, Edward Bates too extreme for others. But Lincoln had offended no faction. Though not the first choice of a great many, he left all "in a mood to come to us, if they shall be compelled to give up their first love." "Do not stir them up to anger," he had advised his supporters. "Keep cool under all circumstances." Furthermore, he lost no occasion to flesh out his yeoman image. At the state convention in Decatur he recalled his stop in the area thirty years earlier, when he had built a cabin, split rails and cultivated a small farm. At that point John Hanks bore into the hall two rails purportedly from a lot split in 1830 and inscribed "Abraham Lincoln, the rail candidate for president in 1860."

Lincoln, who made no compromising statements and had no public record to defend, presented himself as the people's choice — one who could appeal to and understand the masses.

He remained at home while 10,000 citizens crowded into the convention hall nicknamed the Wigwam and 20,000 more waited outside. The place throbbed with negotiation. "We are dealing tenderly with delegates," a telegram informed him. A reply came back to Chicago, "I authorize no bargains and will be bound by none." David Davis grumbled, "Lincoln ain't here and don't know what we have to meet": and the bargaining continued.

Lincoln heeded his own advice; he stayed cool. When word of the nomination came into the telegraph office, he walked home to tell his wife, and the next day he read the platform with approval. Its planks attracted many, offended few: a moderate, carefully adjusted protective tariff; homesteads for yeomen; no immigration restrictions; attacks on proposals to reopen the slave trade and on popular sovereignty; demands for the admission of Kansas as a free state; a paean of praise to the Union, and a denunciation of Democratic corruption and extravagance. On the general issue of slavery in the territories this statement was much more cautious than the Republican platform of 1856. At once Lincoln set to work mending fences. Letters to Chase, Cassius M. Clay, Schuyler Colfax, and others expressed the special need of assistance of all and the unwavering purpose to stand for the right. Thurlow Weed, the New York boss, who stopped in Springfield for a conference, received assurance of fair treatment for the Seward people.

The Democratic convention, as expected, split apart. Douglas had a majority but not the two-thirds needed for the nomination under the party's rule. One wing, meeting in Baltimore, called on him to run. The other, in Richmond, demanded the positive protection of slavery and put forward John C. Breckinridge of Kentucky. Still another group, the Constitutional Union party committed to compromise, nominated John Bell of Tennessee and Edward Everett of Massachusetts. Gerrit Smith, by contrast, bore the standard of uncompromising abolitionism.

Lincoln did not campaign or deliver speeches or issue position papers. He had said what he had to say. He hired two secretaries, John George Nicolay and John Hay, to help with his correspondence, saw visitors, reporters, photographers, and painters. At Greeley's suggestion he agreed to prepare a brief autobiography. The sketch, published jointly by the *Chicago Press and Tribune* and the *New York Tribune,* sold more than a million copies. He responded to requests for autographs, but to none for anything more substantial.

The party united in support of "honest Abe," the rail splitter from Illinois, and exploited his rise from obscurity to fame, from poverty to honorable position. Seward, Bates, and others stumped for him, and Republican Wide Awakes, young men in glazed hats and capes, bearing flaming torches or lamps attached to fence rails, marched in zigzag formation simulating a rail fence. This presidential candidate appealed to the voters not as a general, as Pierce, Taylor, Harrison, and Jackson had; not as former Speaker of the House, as Polk had; not as once vice-president, as John Adams had; and not as former secretary of state, as every other victor had; but as an ordinary citizen, deserving trust by virtue of his very ordinariness.

Douglas, taking southern threats of secession seriously, broke with tradition and actively campaigned in New England, the middle states, and the West as the only candidate able to hold the country together. When large Republican majorities in early state elections persuaded him that Lincoln would win, he headed south determined to save the Union. Damning abolitionists and seceders alike, Douglas argued that election of a Republican would not justify secession.

In the South, however, anti-Lincoln sentiments reached feverish intensity. "Vulgar," "illiterate," "pettifogging," "unqualified" were among the moderate adjectives applied to him. Doubts cast on his legitimacy alternated with aspersions on his patriotism during the Mexican War. Rumors of black uprisings, of wells poisoned in Texas, and of threats to the cotton crop convinced extremists that Lincoln's election would bring slavery to an end. By controlling the patronage he would swamp the South with Republican officeholders of every shape and color. The money-grubbing northerners would stop at nothing. Their "horrid looking" candidate — a "blood thirsty tyrant," a "sooty" and "scoundrelly" creature — and his mulatto running mate, Hannibal Hamlin of Maine, would urge blacks to marry white women and, if denied, to rape them. "What social monstrosities, what desolated fields, what civil broils, what robberies, rapes and murders of the poorer whites by emancipated blacks would then disfigure the whole fair face of this prosperous, smiling and happy Southern land."

Lincoln, unlike Douglas, did not take secessionist sentiments seriously. He had heard this type of muttering before too and judged it an empty threat. The good people of the South, he believed, had too much good sense and good temper to attempt the ruin of the government. The strong unionists in the area would triumph over the fire eaters.

On the night of November 6 Lincoln sat in the telegraph office watching the figures. He received 1,866,452 votes to Douglas's 1,376,957. Breckinridge polled 849,781, and Bell 588,879. Lincoln's three opponents together outvoted him, and although he got a few border state votes he got none at all in the South. The electoral outcome was clear, however — Lincoln, 173; Breckinridge, 73; Bell, 39; and Douglas, 12. Even had his opponents united, Lincoln would still have won. There were no constitutional grounds on which to contest his election.

But on the consequences Douglas was right, Lincoln wrong. All along the Little Giant had warned that Lincoln invited "a war of sections, a war of the North against the South, of the free States against the slave States — a war of extermination." In December South Carolina led the way to secession and thus forced Lincoln, three months before he took office, to contemplate the unhappy problem of how to restore the Union.

VIII

Conflict without End

THE LINCOLNS had come a long way since they had last resided in the nation's capital. It was a sign of improved status that they primed Robert for Harvard. Though he had failed fifteen of the sixteen entrance examinations, a year at Exeter had readied him for college. Mary now discovered within reach the grandeur of which she had long dreamed, and she longed to cram it all in. As for the president-elect, he too prepared a new identity for the new office.

Back in October an eleven-year-old girl had written from Westfield, New York, suggesting that Lincoln grow a beard. Ladies liked whiskers and would "tease their husbands to vote for you." The amused candidate answered that people might think it a silly affectation. Nevertheless he allowed a growth to frame the rugged features of his face.

Early on, the Lincolns learned that the White House was as distant from home as Washington was from Springfield. They suffered personal and family wounds as the penalties of success. The District of Columbia was a southern town, its leading figures for decades drawn from, or modeled on, plantation society. Everyone who was anyone resented the intrusion of the Black Republican; all the couth people iced up at the approach of the uncouth. If the president could shrug off the slights and insults, his neurasthenic wife could not.

Mary set to work redecorating the dilapidated and shabby White House. In frequent trips to Philadelphia and New York she assembled a vast collection of goods and furniture, for she had determined to use the $20,000 appropriated by Congress to show Washington society the excellence of her taste. She bought drapes, oriental carpets, carved furniture, and expensive china — price was no object for the presidential residence. To her personal account she charged elegant gowns, shawls, and boxes of gloves. By Christmas she transformed the White House into an ornate, richly decorated, and well-kept mansion. She herself, dressed according to the latest issue of *Godey's*, acted every inch the first lady.

None of it dissolved her unhappiness. Her husband, occupied with other matters, hardly noticed the changes she had wrought. She missed her friends and made few new ones. Insecure and avid for attention, she allowed flattery and insincerity to sway her. She felt free only with her black seamstress. A life of hardship and disappointment had steeled Elizabeth Keckley against misfortune, and her compassionate manner gave Mary welcome respite from the stiff formality of official duties. The president's wife unburdened herself at fittings and talked of her extravagance, her fears of poverty, her private debts, and her loneliness.

When the bills came in, she discovered to her horror that she had exceeded the appropriation by $6700. When the commissioner of public buildings interceded with Lincoln on her behalf, the president became livid with rage. "It would stink in the nostrils of the American people to have it said the President of the United States had approved a bill overrunning an appropriation of $20,000 for flub dubs for this damned old house, when the soldiers can not have blankets." He would rather pay out of his own pocket. In the end Congress buried an extra appropriation in the next year's budget.

As time went on Mary's personal problems increased and caused embarrassing scenes. Lincoln, understanding her difficulties, remained gently loving and always defended her against detractors. Husband and wife rarely quarrelled, and they supported each other in the hard times. But the stresses under which they labored, even before they entered the White House, now and again erupted in heart-rending scenes.

In the first year the sound of children's voices soothed the spirit. For Willie and Tad the White House offered constant adventure and excitement. Unrestrained by their parents, they roamed the mansion, disturbing conferences, annoying visitors, and assembling a veritable zoo of their pets. Their indulgent father took them to visit the troops along the Potomac and often joined their antics in the back rooms, entering their world and playing in it as an equal. Deeply devoted to them, he found unending delight and relaxation in their presence. Willie was the more serious of the two, a gentle and affectionate child, a bit of a dreamer who loved to read poetry and history. Tad on the other hand resembled his mother — nervous, hyperactive. He suffered from a speech impediment; he was a slow learner but rambunctious and happy; and he easily made friends among the staff.

Secession, party factionalism, patronage seekers, and officious bearers of unsolicited advice had made inauguration week a nightmare. Four months had passed since election, and Lincoln, powerless, had stubbornly held to the policy of inaction. Having already said all there was to say, he resisted all pressures to deliver yet another explanatory pronouncement that southerners might interpret as weakness in the face of threats. To suggestions of a softened position he responded, "Let there be no compromise on the question of extending slavery." The more carefully he considered the problem the more certain he was that "the principle of 'Liberty to all' — the principle that clears the *path* for all — gives *hope* to all — and, by consequence, *enterprize,* and *industry* to all," that principle was the *"apple of gold"* subsequently framed by "the picture of silver" formed by the Union and the Constitution. "The *picture* was made for the apple — *not* the apple for the picture." And indeed in December and January when the Deep South seceded, mediators like John J. Crittenden and the old Whigs who labored for an accommodation discovered that nothing less would satisfy the southerners than a guarantee in perpetuity — of slavery not only where it was but also where it might spread in the Caribbean and elsewhere.

By the time Lincoln had left Springfield for Washington on February 11, 1861, seven states were out, a convention in Montgomery, Alabama, planned a Confederacy, and secessionist flames crackled in the lame-duck Congress. Disappointed by the inability of his friend Alexander H. Stephens to prevent Georgia's withdrawal, the president-elect nevertheless still did nothing. Legally he could do nothing while Buchanan was still chief executive, and Lincoln could not face the prospect that the unthinkable might happen. Virginia and the border states were loyal; he persuaded himself that they, his kind of people, would remain so.

Intimations of Necessity had shadowed the journey to the White House. Rumors of assassination plots and piles of hate mail convinced Seward and General Winfield Scott to map out the route through Northern territory. Masses of Americans for the first time then saw their elected leader, for the train stopped in numerous towns and villages. The party reached New York City on February 18, to learn of Jefferson Davis's inauguration as president of the Confederate States of America. Lincoln seemed much wearied and careworn, dazed and confused. "There is nothing going wrong," he told Columbus, Ohio. "Time, patience and a reliance on that God who has never forsaken his people" would solve the problems. "What is the matter with them?" he asked plaintively in Cleveland. "Why all this excitement? Why all these complaints?" The country would save itself. In his heart Lincoln knew that it would not be so; notes jotted along the way showed his loyalty to past declarations and his determination not to allow the destruction of the Union.

In Philadelphia Allan Pinkerton had informed him of an assassination plot in Baltimore. A letter from Seward confirmed the news: a group had determined to murder him be-

fore he reached Washington. Mary, having learned of the
threat, had plunged into hysterics, and Lincoln, changing
plans, arrived in Washington unobserved and disguised as the
brother of a Pinkerton agent. Opposition papers made much
of "the flight of Abraham." The flood of abuse reached new
levels. One cartoon showed the president-elect's face with a
huge padlock shutting his lips. His escape in Baltimore was
considered unmanly, his manner boorish and crude, his language barbaric, and his wife a backwoods shrew. By March 4
General Scott had received more than 300 threatening letters.
Rumors of southern plans to seize the city and prevent the
inauguration had put the army on the alert. But James Buchanan placidly escorted Lincoln to the Capitol, where the
new president delivered his address.

Lincoln was conciliatory yet firm. To allay southern fears
he guaranteed "the property, peace and security" of every
section. But he held "that in contemplation of universal law
and of the Constitution, the Union of these States is perpetual." Nothing in the Constitution provided for its peaceful
dissolution. No state could lawfully leave the Union, and acts
of violence against the authority of the United States were in-
surrectionary or revolutionary, according to circumstances. A
minority, threatened by majority force, could appeal to the
Constitution and resort to revolution if necessary. But this
clearly was not now the case. The majority wished only to
guard the government against a minority threatening secession,
which meant anarchy and despotism. To accept the rule of
the minority as a permanent arrangement was to accept chaos.
Physically the two sections could never separate, and war
would settle nothing and would cause much loss on both
sides and no gain on either. Then once the fighting ceased,
the identical old questions as to terms of intercourse would
arise again.

Lincoln pleaded for calm, for thought, for patience: "Intelligence, patriotism, Christianity, and a firm reliance on Him
who has never yet forsaken this favored land" might still ease

the present difficulty. The momentous issue of civil war was in the hands not of the president but of dissatisfied fellow countrymen. They had "no oath registered in Heaven to destroy the government," while he was about to take a most solemn one to "preserve, protect and defend" it. The government would not assail them, he added; "We are not enemies, but friends." The bonds of affection endured, "mystic chords of memory, stretching from every battle field and patriot grave, to every living heart and hearthstone, all over this broad land."

Before a fortnight had passed the new administration confronted the crisis at Fort Sumter. Lincoln had drawn into his cabinet not his own supporters but his former opponents, the national Republican leaders. Seward of State, Chase at the Treasury, Bates in Justice had been serious candidates for the 1860 nomination, and service before then as governors or congressmen had deepened their experience. Cameron, at the War Department, was a dubious character but a master of Pennsylvania politics. The family connections of Postmaster Blair reached from Maryland to Missouri, and he himself had been of counsel to *Dred Scott*. Gideon Welles at the Navy and Caleb Smith in Interior brought high competence to their departments and useful party ties to Connecticut and Indiana. The cabinet members had been Free-Soilers or Whigs or Democrats, and they represented all the sections but the Deep South. Some would prove temperamentally conservative, others radical, and each shared in the general assumption that he was the superior of the backwoods president. Indifferent to their condescension toward him and toward one another, Lincoln used them for their abilities, shed Cameron when he could, and kept the others working for him and for the Union.

On March 15 Lincoln learned that Fort Sumter in Charleston harbor, surrounded by rebel batteries, was running out of supplies. To abandon the position would jettison pledges repeatedly made to hold on to federal property everywhere. To employ force might provoke a Southern response and war.

Feverish cabinet consultations and conflicting military advice left Lincoln uncertain. All the troubles and anxieties of his life, he later confided to Orville Browning, were nothing compared to the month that followed. Nevertheless he gently pocketed suggestions from Seward and others to let the best qualified cabinet members handle the emergency for him, and he faced Necessity on its own terms.

When a secret agent informed him that nothing would pacify the rebels short of independence, the president dispatched a supply expedition to the fort. On April 6 a message notified the governor of South Carolina that the fleet would depart shortly. On April 12 rebel fire forced Sumter to yield. Two days later Lincoln told the cabinet that the choice was "immediate dissolution or blood." Without further ado he asked the states to provide 75,000 militiamen for three months' service and called a special session of Congress to meet on July 4. Meanwhile some border states dropped away — Virginia, then Arkansas, then North Carolina, and early in June Tennessee, reluctant to be stranded in a Union in which the free states would far outnumber the slave. Forced now to choose, these states found the southern ties strongest.

Although everyone in Washington knew that the war would soon be over, the president issued a series of proclamations and orders, blockading the southern coast, adding men to the army and navy, calling for 42,034 three-year volunteers, and suspending the writ of habeas corpus. Army commanders behind the lines received the power to impose martial law and to try civilians in military courts.

The nation, however, lacked the basic equipment for war. Understaffed, inexperienced, poorly financed, and badly managed, the federal government slowly, painfully, tackled the enormous mess by trial and error. The cabinet, composed of men jealous of each other, and at first dubious about the president's abilities, often worked at cross purposes, its members interfering in one another's agencies, in the effort to pacify their own constituents.

A sturdy maritime tradition eased the situation at sea. Fewer naval than army commanders went over to the Confederacy, and the merchant fleet, then at its apogee, supplied an effective training ground. Politicians did not assume that commissions were their due, and Lincoln could rely on Secretary Welles for efficient administration of the department.

The president did have to intervene in diplomacy, much as he respected Seward's ability. Great Britain's drift toward recognition of Confederate belligerency infuriated the secretary of state. England, France, and other countries might join in rejecting the American contention that the conflict was but a domestic insurrection. Admission "to the family of nations" would enable the South to seek military alliances and even armed intervention to guarantee her sovereignty. Seward drafted a bold memorandum threatening war unless England accepted the Union blockade and refrained from any intercourse with rebel commissioners. After consulting Senator Charles Sumner, who thought Seward insane, Lincoln deleted the offensive language and sent the memorandum to Ambassador Charles Francis Adams, for his eyes only. London would learn the basic American position but without hostility. Lincoln had no wish to lose Seward's service, but he tactfully set the limits to his secretary of state's impetuosity so that effective diplomacy prevented crises the country could not then handle.

Simon Cameron's War Department was a disaster. It could not possibly deal with the hordes swarming into Washington, expecting somehow to be transformed into a competent fighting force. Nothing was at hand — not shoes or uniforms or guns. "The plain matter of fact," Lincoln wrote, was that our good people "rushed to the rescue of the government faster than the government [could] find arms to put in their hands." Even thoroughly honest and masterfully efficient administrators would have faced a massive job in finding supplies, purchasing them, and getting them to the troops. That this was the first great war in which the railroad and the telegraph often were important only complicated matters, as did the fact that Cameron's people were neither thoroughly honest nor efficient.

The volunteers about to engulf the little regular army made the shortage of trained officers painfully apparent. The plantation way of life and chivalric values encouraged Southerners in military careers. A high proportion of experienced commanders therefore joined the Confederacy. Until Virginia's secession, for instance, Lincoln had counted on the services of Robert E. Lee, who then put loyalty to the state above loyalty to the nation. By contrast many northern West Pointers, swayed by business values, had become civilians during peacetime. U. S. Grant kept a store in Galena, Illinois; George B. McClellan was a railroad official; and William T. Sherman, having tried banking in San Francisco, was a Kansas lawyer. Winfield Scott, the Union army commander — dedicated, competent, popular — had advanced to the rank of general after the Battle of Lundy's Lane in 1814. When Sumter fell, Old Fuss 'n Feathers was about seventy-five years old but the best available.

Washington suffered from no want of applicants for commissions and the titles, uniforms, swords, glory, and political capital that a short war would bring. Any American could fight on land; there seemed no need for the special skills the navy required. Every state demanded its share, with no bar to buffoons, charlatans, and incompetents. And these and other patronage matters consumed much of the president's time. He and the troops would pay the penalty.

"This is essentially a People's contest," Lincoln told the assembled Congress on July 4, 1861. The Union fought for a government that would "elevate the condition of men" and give all "a fair chance, in the race of life." Those who could win elections could also suppress a rebellion. "When ballots have fairly and constitutionally decided, there can be no successful appeal, except to ballots themselves, at succeeding elections." And upon the fate of the Union hung the fate of world democracy.

"On to Richmond" became the popular rallying cry. The folks at home egged on the unorganized and undisciplined troops that flooded Washington in the expectation of a quick lark in thrashing Johnny Reb. Many a former pacifist among the abolitionists flamed in bellicosity with awareness that the battle was the Lord's and set forth in anger to seize the Confederate capital and trample out secession. Victory now might also be the means of extirpating slavery.

Again and again the demand for a quick, decisive end to the war thrust the troops into disaster. On the morning of July 22, 1861, Lincoln viewed the survivors straggling back to Washington from Bull Run, covered with mud and soaked by the steadily falling rain, without knapsacks, crossbelts, or firelocks. Some were covered only with blankets. In the woeful years that followed, the sight became familiar throughout the land.

Lincoln too had wanted a swift return to peace to avoid damage, ease the strain on the loyalty of the remaining border states, and restore constitutional government. Excessive expectations and initial defeat shook the country's confidence in him and his own faith in himself. Horace Greeley, who suffered no such self-doubts, reported, "You are not considered a great man" and urged him to sign an armistice with the rebels.

An armistice was a defeat for freedom and for the Union. The quick hammer blow had failed. Sadly the president came to understand the virtues and the costs of Scott's anaconda policy — surround the South and squeeze it to death. Lincoln resolved to tighten the blockade, enroll fresh troops for longer service, and push three expeditions simultaneously into Virginia, into East Tennessee, and down the Mississippi.

Months elapsed indecisively. Lincoln gave command of the Army of the Potomac to George B. McClellan, a West Point graduate, a veteran of the Mexican War, and a superb organizer but also vain, opinionated, and politically ambitious. "Little Mack" responded to the plea to save the nation but determined to do it in his own way and for his own ends. He would create an irresistible fighting force, then in one crushing drive take Richmond so that he could dictate a peace that would bring the South back in return for a guarantee of slavery. Doggedly he took his time in preparation, shaking off the criticism of congressmen chafing at delay, drift, and debacle.

In January 1862 Lincoln made up his mind. War had its own imperatives. The people were impatient, the treasury empty, and the generals ill. The bottom was out of the tub. He determined to reorganize the War Department, take the initiative in the field, and recognize the altered objectives of the war.

As he acted, personal tragedy struck. Willie and Tad came down with fevers. There were optimistic phrases from the physician. Tad recovered. Willie lingered, and his parents could do little but observe his suffering, sitting with him in the night, bathing his face as he tossed, turned, and cried. His condition worsened and his death on February 20, 1862, overwhelmed Lincoln with grief. Mary collapsed. She could not attend the funeral and for weeks would not leave her room. She suffered a nervous breakdown and for three months refused to go out.

Unable to bear the memory of her dear Willie, she gave away all his toys and attended few official functions. Religion provided some solace, as did seances and spiritualism. Mary eagerly grasped the opportunity mediums offered to communicate with her dead child. To bury her sorrow by sharing the suffering of others, she visited hospitals, distributing food and flowers to wounded soldiers.

But her instability deepened, as black moods alternated with more hopeful periods, only to be broken by temper tantrums and headaches. She worried about her husband's health, his safety, and his happiness. Recognizing his private way of suffering, so different from her own, Mary tried to take him to some of the seances with her, and occasionally he went, to please her. He comforted his distraught wife as best he could, but as the costs of war mounted he spoke more often of God, in a more intimate, less impersonal way than formerly. "I have all my life been a fatalist," he told a visitor one day. Acceptance of Necessity, a force beyond human control, helped Lincoln in his darker hours. He began to glimpse himself as a man placed where he was for purposes higher than he could presently see. Meanwhile work provided a welcome release and distraction.

Mismanagement, corruption, misappropriations, and sheer incompetence in the War Department hampered the army. Rotten blankets, knapsacks that came apart in the rain, and fraudulent contracts were matters of common knowledge. Lincoln shuffled Cameron off to Russia as United States minister and appointed in his place Edwin M. Stanton, until then Cameron's chief legal advisor. Stanton had openly abused Lincoln in the recent past. It just did not pay to carry a grudge, Lincoln said. Stanton was the best man for the job. Incorruptible, he had had government experience and knew how to manage the department. He worked hard and drove everyone else to work as hard. And he, like Lincoln, had tired of McClellan's delays. "This army has got to fight," he said; "the champagne and oysters on the Potomac must be stopped."

Lincoln ordered the Army of the Potomac to march on Richmond by way of Manassas, with simultaneous operations by all units in Kentucky, on the Mississippi, and in the Gulf of Mexico. McClellan, however, had a plan of his own, not a frontal but a flanking attack that would not only strike at Richmond but also cut the rebels off, take all Virginia, crush the Deep South, and end the rebellion. Although Lincoln deferred to his experience, McClellan continued to procrastinate. His behavior, said Seward and Chase, had been imbecilic; and Bates sternly told Lincoln that it was his presidential duty to "command the commanders." By now Lincoln had come to know his general as a brilliant organizer and administrator but one who lost his nerve on the eve of battle.

In May and June 1862 McClellan led his forces up the peninsula between the James and York rivers toward Richmond. Two months of inconclusive fighting produced no results, only new demands. McClellan wanted 100,000 more men and six more weeks before he would march on Richmond.

The public did not see it his way. The Republicans running in local elections clamored for McClellan's dismissal to stave off their expected electoral defeat. By then the issue was political as well as military. It involved not only the choice of a general and a decision about tactics but also the definition of the war's purpose — whether to fight for McClellan's limited objectives or for the broader ones sought by influential elements in the Republican party. These considerations added weight to accusations of timidity against the general. Back in May, Lincoln, Chase, and Seward had sailed to the peninsula to find out what went on. The president himself had ordered an attack on Norfolk, which promptly fell. Perhaps only the will to win was lacking.

Lincoln tried briefly to alter the structure of command, but a second defeat at Bull Run plunged him into despair. "We are whipped again," he told Hay, and he feared that the war was lost. He saw no alternative but to restore McClellan's sole command despite furious objections from Stanton, Chase, and other cabinet members. To Bates, Lincoln, "wrung by the bitterest anguish" had exclaimed that he "felt almost ready to hang himself." But the president stuck to his decision to fall back on McClellan.

Alone in the White House Lincoln pondered the meaning of his and the nation's suffering. God had a purpose that mortal weaklings could not fathom. But what was that purpose? And which side in the contest was right when it invoked the will of God? "God can not be for and against the same thing at the same time." And conceivably God's purpose differed from the purposes of the two parties, both just "instrumentalities," behaving as they did because He wanted it so. God had clearly willed this contest and just as clearly had determined not to have it end yet. By his power He could either have "saved or destroyed the union without human contest." Yet blood was shed. And when He pleased, the war would be over. But only He knew when that would be.

In these lonely reflections, "God" had replaced "Necessity," the word the president earlier had used. Brooding as before, overwhelmed by personal and national tragedy, he now preferred the traditional term, although confronting the one as the other, he saw only a blank.

Having chosen McClellan, Lincoln had to strengthen the commitment he was already making about the war objectives. He could not, as Greeley had counseled, consider an armistice, nor could he, as McClellan wished, revert to the condition of 1860, with a guarantee of slavery. The Union could not endure half-slave, half-free. Since Lincoln had spoken those memorable words, experience had demonstrated their profound validity. Yet neither could the president take such rash steps as might alienate the loyal slave states from Delaware to Missouri. The only tolerable policy was one that would set the nation on the road toward ultimate emancipation without endangering the Union. To develop such a policy Lincoln had to avoid the uncomprehending, obstinate crossfire from narrow-minded abolitionists on the one hand and fanatical slaveholders on the other.

In the early summer of 1861 General John Charles Frémont had taken charge of the western department, headquartered in St. Louis. On August 30 he had placed Missouri under martial law and declared slaves of rebels free men. Although he went far beyond the Confiscation Act passed by Congress he became an abolitionist hero. Aware of the strain on Union strength in the border states, Lincoln requested repeal of the proclamation. Frémont refused. Thereupon the president ordered the general to leave political decisions to Congress and to revise the slave provisions.

Abolitionists responded furiously. Sumner branded Lincoln a virtual dictator, who behaved, Senator Benjamin F. Wade declared, like one "born of poor white trash and educated in a slave state." Emancipation leagues in Northern cities set about reversing the proslavery policies born of the president's "pig headed stupidity." The imperious Jessie Benton Frémont steamed into a midnight interview and warned the president not to dare interfere with her husband. Meanwhile, everything in the west, military and financial, sank into hopeless confusion as waste and corruption engulfed the command. In October 1861 Lincoln dismissed the general, getting the message through by an emissary disguised as a farmer. Taken by surprise, Frémont, not half the man his wife was, acquiesced. But the cavalier treatment of their hero further alienated the abolitionists.

Pressure in favor of an emancipation proclamation mounted. It was absurd to fight without removing the slavery that had caused the war. Eradication of the institution would weaken the South and, Sumner said, might well prevent Great Britain from recognizing the Confederacy. But Lincoln knew that the border states had maintained their precarious loyalty to the Union out of confidence that he would not interfere with their domestic institutions. It would do no good to free the slaves on paper only, then lose the war.

Gradual emancipation, based on federal compensation for every slave freed, was the only way out. At first the president had hoped to experiment in Delaware with a plan to free the small slave population over a period of thirty years in return for $500 a head. The federal government could also try to colonize blacks either in Liberia or Central America. No Delaware legislator would sponsor the plan, however.

On December 3, 1861, Lincoln's annual message to Congress urged the appropriation of federal funds for colonization. But he refused to issue any proclamation that would convert the

conflict into "a violent and remorseless revolutionary struggle."
Although the government would use all measures to prosecute
the war successfully, it would not drift into radical and extreme measures, which would harm the loyal as well as the
disloyal. Out of diffidence to border state sensibilities he also
had approved the employment of blacks as foragers and laborers, but not as soldiers.

Now, in the spring of 1862, during the dark season of brooding after Willie's death, during the mournful reappraisals of
defeats in the field, Lincoln's priorities subtly shifted. Border
state support was still vital. But, he told Senator Sumner, the
war was a great movement of God to end slavery, and "the
man would be a fool who should stand in the way." In March
the president suggested a compensated emancipation plan to
Congress. The rebellion might make measures previously considered extreme indispensable to ending the struggle.

The message created a furor. The *New York Tribune* hailed
it as "the day star of a new dawn." Lincoln assured congressmen from the sensitive border states that the property of every
loyal Southerner would remain untouched, but most of them
voted against it when Congress subsequently approved the
measure. Lincoln also signed laws forbidding Union officers
to return fugitive slaves to the Confederacy and abolishing
slavery in the District of Columbia, with compensation to the
owners and funds for colonization. Furthermore, despite the
Dred Scott judgment, a statute outlawed slavery in the territories. However, Lincoln revoked a proclamation of emancipation similar to Frémont's, issued by General David Hunter for
the coastal islands off South Carolina.

Trumbull, Sumner, and various other abolitionists and Republicans urged more decisive action. But Lincoln was adamant: "I can only go just as fast as I can see how I go." And
for the time being, in the absence of favorable military news,
he still needed support from the border states. On July 12,
1862, he explained that the war had made human bondage in-
compatible with restoration of the Union. Acceptance of grad-

ual emancipation would have extinguished all Confederate hopes that the border states would ultimately join the rebellion. Now slavery everywhere was doomed "by mere friction and abrasion . . . by the mere incidents of the war," and masters would have nothing to show for it unless they shortened the conflict by a decision at once to emancipate gradually and for compensation. There was plenty of room in South America for colonization, and, once the slaves happily settled there, free Negroes would join them too.

The border state representatives disregarded the appeal. The federal government did not have enough money for emancipation, and liberation in any form would consolidate the spirit of rebellion in the South and fan secession sentiment among loyal slaveholders from Delaware to Missouri. Similar complaints reached Lincoln from Louisiana. To all such allies who felt betrayed Lincoln responded that he distrusted "the wisdom if not the sincerity of friends who would hold my hands while my enemies stab me." The appeal "of professed friends has paralyzed me more in this struggle than any other one thing." He was patient, and what he could not do he would not. But it was his duty to save the government, and he wished it understood, once for all, that he would not surrender the game leaving any available card unplayed. When appeals to sense of responsibility, to American ideals, and to self-interest failed, he concluded that slaveowners, even those loyal to the Union, would not voluntarily part with their human property.

The same conclusion emerged from the earliest efforts to reconstruct the slave states captured by federal forces. "The paralysis — the dead palsy — of the government in this whole struggle" derived from the unwillingness of the Union men in rebel states to do anything except demand that "the government shall not strike its open enemies, lest they be struck by accident." The army needed men and money and could get neither if it drove slaves from its lines. The people of Louisiana who wished to protect their persons and property had only to set up a state government in conformity with the Constitution. The army would then withdraw. But their response was selfish, and the president would not surrender the government to save them from losing all. One could not prosecute a war "with elder stalk squirts, charged with rose water." To August Belmont, he explained that broken eggs could not be mended, but Louisiana could take "her place in the Union as it was, barring the already broken eggs." The sooner she did so, the smaller the amount past mending. The government could not much longer play "a game in which it stakes all and its enemies stake nothing." The enemies of the Union had to understand that they could not experiment for ten years trying to destroy the government and still come back unhurt if they failed. If they had any expectation ever to enter the Union as it was, now was the time.

When the South remained obdurate, the response of the president was emancipation, directed at those who most deserved punishment and would suffer the most by it. Slavery was at the root of rebellion. As a "last and only alternative . . . a military necessity, absolutely essential to the preservation of the union," Lincoln would ask the slaves, whose very presence aided the southern cause, to desert and join the Union forces as free men. But since he knew the opposition such a measure would encounter, he preferred to let Congress enact a second confiscation law, which took away the slaves of rebels found guilty by federal courts and appropriated $500,000 for colonization. Even that measure, some Republicans and Democrats feared, violated the rules of "civilized warfare."

Through the summer of 1862 Lincoln also dealt with demands for immediate abolition — somehow. Horace Greeley, who only a year earlier had offered the South a guarantee of slavery in return for an armistice, now breathed fiery righteousness. In an open letter, published under the title "The Prayer of Twenty Millions," he accused the president of evading the new Confiscation Act, under the influence of "certain fossil politicians" from the border states. The Union cause suffered from undue "deference to Rebel Slavery." The nation demanded "a frank, declared, unqualified, ungrudging execution of the laws of the land." Charles Sumner, involved in a difficult fight for reelection in Massachusetts, also pressed for immediate action.

Lincoln refused to budge and counseled patience and moderation. Time, he told everyone, was essential. On August 22, 1862, he published a reply to his old friend Greeley, whose heart, all knew, was always in the right place. Lincoln agreed that the Union should be saved. But he disagreed with those who would not save it without at the same time destroying slavery. Union, not slavery, was at stake. "If I could save the Union without freeing any slaves I would do it, and if I could save it by freeing all the slaves, I would do it, and if I could save it by freeing some and leaving others alone, I would also do that."

The president did not tell Greeley what the cabinet had confidentially learned a month earlier: that he intended to abolish rebel slavery by executive fiat and thus avoid tangled litigation in the courts. A draft of a preliminary emancipation proclamation stated that on January 1, 1863, as commander in chief, he would liberate all slaves in the rebellious states, those of secessionists and loyalists alike. The destruction of slavery in the Confederate South was a fit and necessary military measure to ensure the salvation of the Union. Some cabinet members had dissented, but Lincoln had made the decision. He replied to Greeley as he did not out of uncertainty but to mobilize the maximum support for emancipation when the time came. At the moment, the Union forces had not won a clear military victory. Skeptics in Europe and in the United States might view the step as a desperate measure to provoke a slave insurrection in the South. Riots revealed rising anti-Negro sentiments in the North, and he did not want the proclamation to appear a maneuver to cover up the ineptitude of his generals.

He proceeded also to prepare the nation by talking extensively of colonization. Desirable as he believed black migration ultimately to be, he knew there was no realistic prospect of an immediate removal of the former slaves. Still, discussion of the possibility might make freedom more palatable. On August 14 in the White House he read Negro leaders an address on the subject. "You and we are different races," he told the delegation. "This physical difference is a great disadvantage to us both." The blacks in America suffered terrible injustices and they would never be truly free in a white man's country. They had to face this fact of life. But whites suffered too in a bloody war, not knowing how it would all end, and without slavery "and the colored race as a basis, the war could not have an existence." The black leaders had to make clear to their people that removal was the only solution. Negroes who refused to move took "an extremely selfish view of the case." His audience then heartily endorsed his position, although Frederick Douglass blasted the president for "his inconsistencies, his pride of race and blood, his contempt for negroes and his canting hypocrisy."

In response to a memorial from a public meeting of several Christian denominations in Chicago on September 13, 1862, Lincoln rehearsed all the objections to national emancipation. His word alone would not free anyone; he could not even enforce the Constitution in the rebel states. And what would happen to slaves once free? "How can we feed and care for such a multitude?" There were not enough arms to equip the white troops; how could one spare some for the blacks? And there was a good chance that the border states might go over to the Confederacy. A general proclamation at the moment was "like the Pope's bull against the comet." The president admitted that emancipation would mobilize northern and world sympathy and would strike at the heart of Southern power, depriving the section of laborers. "The subject is on my mind, by day and night, more than any other," he added. "Whatever shall appear to be God's will I will do."

Within the week the sign came, with news of the battle at Antietam Creek. Lincoln had waited eagerly for the final knockout blow that would destroy the Confederate army under Robert E. Lee. The outcome was not as decisive as the president wished. McClellan had not routed Lee; he had merely halted the advance toward Pennsylvania. But Antietam was a victory.

On September 22, Lincoln read the cabinet a chapter from Artemus Ward's *A High Handed Outrage in Utica*. When Artemus showed up in Utica with a cage full of "wax figures of the Lord's last supper," a fellow pulled Judas out and exclaimed, "What did you bring this pussylanerous cuss here fur?" "You egrajus ass," Artemus replied, "That air's a wax figger — a representation of the false 'postle." The fellow yelled back, that Judas could not appear in "Utiky with impunerty" and destroyed the figure's head. Furious, Artemus "sood" the man, and the jury returned a verdict of "Arson in the 3rd degree."

The cabinet, expecting a historic occasion, did not see the point. Then, as buffoonery eased the terrible, earnest tension under which he labored, Lincoln revealed that he had made a vow to move forward in the cause of emancipation when a McClellan victory proved "an indication of Divine Will" in which God had "decided the question in favor of the slaves." The moment had come. If the seceding states did not return to the Union by January 1, 1863, he would "thenceforward and forever" free all slaves in the rebel states. He would also push for gradual, compensated emancipation in the loyal states and would continue the colonization effort. Human freedom "thenceforward and forever" became a Union rallying cry.

On the first day of the new year, after a sleepless night, Lincoln put the final touches on the proclamation. Admonishing the liberated to refrain from violence, to remain in the South, and to work for reasonable wages, he invoked "the considerate judgment of mankind and the gracious favor of Almighty God" on "an act of justice, warranted by the Constitution" and by military necessity. He signed the document that afternoon after the annual New Year reception, at which Mary appeared for the first time since Willie's death. Visibly nervous and tired, he carefully wrote out his full name, abandoning for the occasion the A. Lincoln he ordinarily used. "If my name ever goes into history it will be for this act," he said.

The events of the preceding year and those of the six months that followed taught the president much about Necessity. If he still did not fathom its meaning fully, he had at least learned to describe its contours. In the hours of waiting for dispatches or of poring over maps and troop dispositions in the War Department, in the moments saved for Mary and for Tad, the words came to mind — stripped of ornament and sabre-sharp — to describe a reality his countrymen recognized.

The Confiscation Act and emancipation had infuriated Northerners unwilling to fight for "nigger" freedom. The Democrats in 1862 had campaigned to save the Union as it was, against the abolitionist dictator, and the most populous northern states returned Democrats to Congress. Yet Lincoln rejected even friendly urgings that he alter his policy. "I am a slow walker," he said, "but I never walk back." Sympathizers had indeed responded to the proclamation "sufficiently in breath, but breath alone kills no rebels."

A draft instituted in March 1863 to deal with recurrent shortages met widespread resistance. A peace movement took form, attacking every aspect of Lincoln's tyrannical presidency — conscription, military arrests, suspension of the writ of habeas corpus, and the Emancipation Proclamation.

The Republicans branded dissidents disloyal, charging the poisonous Copperheads with obstructing the draft, aiding the Confederacy, and killing government agents. Lincoln and Stanton empowered provost marshals to jail anyone who helped the rebellion; more than 13,000 people crowded Northern prisons. Nevertheless, Major John Key was not the only Union officer who maneuvered to prevent a victory, in order to exhaust both armies, "when we will make a compromise and save slavery."

Lincoln concurred in the arrest and imprisonment for the duration of the war of Clement L. Vallandigham, an Ohio

Democrat who advocated a negotiated peace with the Confederacy. "Must I shoot a simple-minded soldier boy who deserts while I must not touch a hair of a wiley agitator who induces him to desert?" And he refused to suspend the draft or revoke the Emancipation Proclamation at the request of Governor Horatio Seymour of New York in the summer of 1863, after draft riots led to orgies of violence, slaughter, burning, and looting. "Are we degenerate?" he wondered. "Has the manhood of our race run out?"

And all the while fighting continued with no end in sight. One general followed another, and victories and losses; still the armies shuttled across Virginia. If Burnside and Hooker failed at Fredericksburg and Chancellorsville to break through to Richmond, Lee had no more success at Antietam and Gettysburg in breaking through to Pennsylvania. And the death toll mounted. For two years, since news of Edward Baker's death at Ball's Bluff had brought tears to his eyes, the president had watched the lengthening lists of the dead and wounded. And asked, Why?

Words took form to express his brooding thoughts about Necessity. To Eliza P. Gurney, an English Quaker, he explained that in the nation's "fiery trial" he tried to do God's work, not always sure what that work was. Had he had his way, "this war would never have been commenced"; had he had his way, "this war would have been ended before this, but we find it still continues and we must believe that He permits it for some wise purpose of his own, mysterious and unknown to us."

Lincoln's address to Congress in December 1862 named that moving power (once Necessity, then God) by another word. Since the *Dred Scott* decision and the debates with Douglas he had spent hours reading *Elliot's Debates on the Federal Constitution, The Annals of Congress* and the *Congressional Globe,* and other works in which he sought the sources of national difficulties as well as of national strength. Necessity by now he sometimes identified with history.

"The dogmas of the quiet past," inadequate to the stormy present, demanded that Americans "rise with the occasion." "As our case is new, so we must think anew, and act anew." It was the great misfortune of his generation to live with the results of the past. "Fellow citizens, *we* can not escape history." Those who held the power bore the responsibility. "In *giving* freedom to the *slave, we assure* freedom to the *free* — honorable alike in what we give and what we preserve. We shall nobly save, or meanly lose, the last best, hope of earth."

Now, on November 19, 1863, he came to mark the opening of a military cemetery in Gettysburg where, four months before, 170,000 Americans had clashed in battle and left 51,000 casualties. He intended to make a concise statement about the larger meaning of the war. Some 15,000 relatives of the fallen, as well as anxious politicians, publicity seekers, and notables had assembled for the occasion. From where he sat in the brilliant sunshine, while Edward Everett droned on for two hours, Lincoln could see beyond the graves the ravaged beauty of the countryside. When the time came, he rose, took the manuscript from his pocket, put on his steel-rimmed glasses, and spoke.

Four score and seven years ago — the tone was scriptural, the rhythm familiar to every reader of the King James Version. The date eighty-seven years before was 1776.

Our fathers — an appeal to the patriarchs as in the Lyceum a quarter-century earlier.

Brought forth on this continent a new nation — the newness of which consisted of its conception in liberty and its dedication to human equality.

We are met on a great battlefield — of a war, *testing whether any nation so conceived and so dedicated can long endure.* It was altogether fitting and proper to dedicate a portion of that battlefield as a final resting-place for those who gave their lives that the nation might live.

Thus far the flow of words followed the pattern of somber reassurance anticipated at the graveside. Now, however, the startled audience heard an unexpected caesura, which Lincoln so clearly intended as a full stop that between the first and second drafts of the speech he introduced a paragraph break at that point.

But in a larger sense, we can not dedicate — we can not consecrate — we can not hallow — this ground.

The explanation follows — *The brave men, living and dead, who struggled here, have consecrated it, far above our poor power to add or detract. The world will little note nor long remember what we say here, but it can never forget what they did here.*

The question just forming in the audience — Why then do 15,000 of us stand here in attendance? — swiftly receives its answer. *It is for us the living, rather, to be dedicated here to the unfinished work which they who fought here have thus far so nobly advanced. It is rather for us to be here dedicated to the great task remaining before us — that from these honored dead we take increased devotion to that cause for which they gave the last full measure of devotion.*

As to the mode of rededication, in hundreds of revivals and reform meetings, the call was familiar though never so eloquent — *that we here highly resolve that these dead shall not have died in vain — that this nation, under God, shall have a new birth of freedom.*

From rebirth in the fiery trial of battle would spring the assurance *that government of the people, by the people, for the people, shall not perish from the earth.*

I X

Victory Denied

THOUGH HE FOLLOWED the Pinkertons' advice, Lincoln had shrugged off fears of assassination on the inaugural trip to Washington in 1861. Yet even then dark forebodings clouded his thoughts.

As the months passed, hundreds of threatening letters crossed his desk. He nevertheless led an open life, ever exposed, unprotected. Passionate hatred lapped around him after the Emancipation Proclamation and even more so after the draft and the prosecution of the Copperheads. The approach of the election of 1864 amplified the hostility from slaveholders and abolitionists, from frustrated office seekers, from Democrats, and from Republicans for whom he was either too radical or too conservative. As election day approached, a Democratic newspaper in Wisconsin trusted that if he were "elected to misgovern for another four years" some bold hand would "pierce his heart with dagger point for the public good." Faithful Ward Lamon came east from Illinois to guard his friend through the nights.

The president had entered his fifty-sixth year when he took the oath of office for a second time. He had visibly aged; he was haggard, with brow constantly furrowed. To his wife he seemed brokenhearted and exhausted. He drove himself hard, wry humor his only regular relief. In 1863, when both he and Tad came down with what physicians diagnosed as smallpox, Lincoln quipped, "Where are now the office seekers?" At last he had something he could give to everyone.

A year later, when Assistant Postmaster General Alexander
W. Randall and Judge Joseph T. Mills called, nothing the
president told them came as a surprise; his appearance and
manner did. They suggested that he take a three-week vacation. Tired and gaunt, he replied that it would do no good.
Thoughts about the welfare of the country would always pur-
sue him.

He was not the "pleasant joker" his reputation made him
out to be but "a man of deep convictions and an unutterable
yearning for the success of the Union cause." His voice was
pleasant, his behavior kind and gentle. As Randall and Mills
listened, they could not help but feel that his mind matched
his body in stature, that they "stood in the presence of the
great guiding intellect of the age and those huge Atlantian
shoulders were fit to bear the weight of the mightiest monar-
chies." His "transparent honesty, his republican simplicity, his
gushing sympathy for those who offered their lives for their
country, his utter forgetfulness of self in his concern for his
country" inspired enormous confidence and the certainty that
"he was Heaven's instrument to conduct his people thro this
red sea of blood to a Canaan of peace and freedom."

The tone changed when Lincoln entertained his visitors
with reminiscences of the past. He recalled the joking during
the great debates of 1858 and told them that as time passed
the seriousness of the theme had excluded banter. By then the
president was full of good spirit, scattering his repartee in all
directions. "It is such social tête-à-tête among friends that enabled Mr. Lincoln to endure mental toils and application that
would crush any other man."

By inauguration time Lincoln's health was failing. Orville
Browning, who saw him in late February, thought he looked
badly and felt badly — apparently more depressed than at any
time since he became president. He was unwell, Lincoln admitted to Joshua Speed who came for a visit: "My feet and
hands always cold, I suppose I ought to be in bed." Rumors of
assassination and abduction again fluttered through the capital,
and Stanton assigned extra guards to protect the president.

On March 14, soon after the inauguration, the cabinet met in Lincoln's bedroom; utterly exhausted, he lay propped up on pillows. Greeley, who appeared for an interview the next week, noted his face "haggard with care, tempest tossed and weatherbeaten," and Secretary Welles observed how worn down the president was.

On election night of 1864 Lincoln had recalled a dream. At about half past two in the morning after a small supper in the White House, he told friends who waited with him for the results about a similar wait four years earlier. He had gone home tired in 1860, and had stretched out on the sofa. Opposite from where he lay was a large mirror, in which he saw himself full length. The glass bore two distinct images of his face, one nearly covering the other. He got up to study the reflection and saw only one perfect image. But when he again reclined the illusion returned, with one face paler and more haggard than the other. Troubled, he told Mary, and, terribly upset, she read into the reflections the meaning that Lincoln would serve two terms but would not live through the second.

In May 1864, while a fierce battle had raged in the Wilderness, Lincoln had scarcely slept for four nights on end. He paced his office and the War Department corridors, anxiously awaiting news from Grant's headquarters. "I must have some relief from this terrible anxiety . . . or it will kill me." Thereupon he went to the opera, although he scarcely listened to the music.

So on April 14, 1865, Abraham Lincoln attended Laura Keene's performance of *Our American Cousin* at Ford's Theater. A little after 10 P.M. John Wilkes Booth arrived in the box to deliver the fatal bullet. The crime occurred on Good Friday — the final gesture of that Necessity in which its victim always believed.

"This war is eating my life out," Lincoln had told Owen Lovejoy, when the worst was already over. "I have a strong impression that I shall not live to see the end."

No victory but had its bitter aftertaste. Gettysburg had removed any further threat that the fighting might shift to northern territory, and probably it had closed the last possibility that Britain might recognize the Confederacy. But the Union army's slowness in pursuit had allowed Lee to escape. "We had them within our grasp," the president groaned. "We had only to stretch forth our hands and they were ours." Distressed immeasurably by loss of the golden opportunity, he feared that "the war will be prolonged indefinitely." As General Meade settled in, "watching the enemy as fast as he can," Lincoln knew that he had not yet found an adequate commander.

In the West the men for that job were in the making — broody failures, with no romantic illusions. Hiram U., called by error Ulysses S., as a boy had hated hunting and killing animals; as a man Grant hated war, hence had left the army for peacetime pursuits. William Tecumseh Sherman, reared in a stranger's family, had also left the military and also knew that war was hell. Both officers answered the call to serve but never deceived themselves into believing that any good would come of fighting except its speedy termination. Mathematically minded, they estimated the odds, calculated what a victory would cost, and, expecting no miracles, paid the price.

Brutally, doggedly, Grant had fought his way from Illinois through Tennessee into Mississippi. The bloody battle of Shiloh alone cost him 13,000 of his 63,000 men. When he took Vicksburg on July 4, 1863, after a six-month siege, he severed the last Confederate link with the West. To a delegation indignant about Grant's drinking problem, Lincoln replied that if he but knew the general's brand, he would send every other commander a barrel of the whiskey.

That autumn Sherman undertook to destroy the southern economy. After consolidating his forces in southern Tennessee, he spent the winter in preparation and then, from Chattanooga, moved southeast to Atlanta, which fell on September 2, 1864. He went on to the sea, destroying fields and wrecking railroads. War was war and not popularity seeking. For several weeks there was no news, and Lincoln hurried often to the

War Department. "I know what hole he went in at but I can't tell what hole he will come out of." Finally on December 10 came word that Sherman had reached the sea, and on Christmas Day 1864 the president received as a present the city of Savannah.

Grant, now commander of all the Union armies, meanwhile pounded away at Lee's forces, pressing on whenever resistance slowed the advance toward Richmond. "I propose to fight it out on this line if it takes all summer," he informed the president. Any other general, Lincoln told Hay, would have fallen back. "It is the dogged pertinacity of Grant that wins." But total casualties in the heavy month of fighting the Wilderness campaign mounted up to 54,000 killed and wounded. Lincoln, glimpsing the maimed and the dead brought into town as he rode out to the Soldier's Home, muttered about "those poor fellows . . . this suffering . . . this loss of life."

Spotsylvania and Cold Harbor added to the toll of "poor fellows." Petersburg fell after a long siege, and Richmond's fate was then sealed. The Confederates clung to their capital until April 3, 1865. Then, with Sherman laying waste the southern heartland in a rapid northward advance through South Carolina, came the final surrender at Appomattox Courthouse on April 9 — five days before Good Friday.

The cost had been staggering — 360,000 Union dead, 260,000 Confederates — all Americans.

To Lincoln the numbers were not abstractions. In those days the president slept little. Often in the gray morning hours he walked across the White House lawn to hail a passing newsboy. He had already done at least an hour's work before breakfast at eight. Then followed another hour at his desk in a simply furnished office in the east wing. Before long, visitors piled in — always too many, because Lincoln wished to make himself accessible. He put them all at ease and listened carefully, hands clasped around his knee, or with one elbow on his knee to support his arms as he stroked his chin. Never entirely passive, he always responded, and if not directly to the point, then with stories, witticisms, and anecdotes so finely mingled that few noticed the digressions. The old cheerful laugh was gone but not the proverbial store of tales and jokes. One visitor felt in the presence of a slightly humorous but thoroughly practical and sagacious backwoodsman and yet also of a statesman whose "abstract and serious eyes" looked out from "an inner sanctuary of thought, sitting in judgment on the scene and feeling its far reach into the future."

Private citizens came in, often unannounced, and consumed precious time. One day Nicolay entered with word of the arrival of the secretary of war, only to discover a group of Quakers holding a prayer meeting while the president bore "the affliction until the spirit moved them to stop." Although his secretaries tried to shield him from physically exhausting, unnecessary burdens, he would not give up the "public opinion baths" that brought him close to the people he governed.

At about one o'clock he made his way to the living quarters, through a corridor still jammed with people waiting to see him. Stops to chat prolonged this process, until 1864, when a door cut into his office gave him direct access to the family apartment. On Tuesdays and Fridays the cabinet met regularly at noon. On Mondays receptions from one to two often left no time for lunch. In the afternoon he read for a while — Shakespeare, Burns, or funny stories — or a servant came in to shave his upper lip and trim the beard, but soon he was back at work. First he signed thousands of commissions, then reviewed all court martial sentences — amounting to some 30,000 in a year. Those involving the death sentence received his closest attention. On a humid day in July, according to John Hay, Lincoln spent six hours on such work, trying his utmost to spare anyone the death penalty, especially soldiers accused of cowardice — "leg cases" he called them, when told of yet another boy who had run away in the face of battle.

During the morning the secretaries sorted the mail, threw away threatening or abusive letters, marked others to go to departments, and sent the rest to the president — usually with the notation "personal" or "political," along with a brief summary written on the envelopes. Lincoln answered as many as he could. His filing system was similar to that he had used as an Illinois lawyer — pigeonholes in a tall desk, marked alphabetically, with separate compartments for cabinet members and a few generals — and Horace Greeley.

Mary Lincoln insisted on fresh air at least once a day. Regularly, weather permitting, the president and his wife took a short ride, often stopping at some hospital to greet the wounded. Dinner followed at six. Once a week, except in the summer, an evening reception or levee brought people by the hundreds to shake his hand and perhaps slip in a request. Lincoln was as disheveled as always, in spite of his wife's efforts. On evenings free of functions he returned to work, with a trip to the War Department telegraph office usually the day's last chore.

Unable to wrench himself away from the particularities of the war, Lincoln shared the suffering of all who appealed to him. He cut through red tape, limited harsh authority, and granted clemency whenever possible. All the department heads soon learned that Lincoln sent over petitioners to rectify injustice or simply to help the needy. The wife of Captain John S. Struthers wanted her husband to resign. Mrs. Hannah Armstrong wanted her sick son discharged. After his mother's appeal, a stay of execution then a pardon saved seventeen-year-old John Murphy, about to be shot for desertion. "Let it be done," Lincoln wrote to Stanton when Abigail C. Berea, whose husband and son had lost their lives in the war, requested the discharge of her youngest boy in poor health. She herself worked as a nurse without pay and was willing to continue, as was a third son in the service.

The president could not limit mercy to the deserving. The Sothoron family complained that they were on the verge of starvation, imprisoned in their house because a relative had shot a Union lieutenant and fled. "Some attention better be given to the case," Lincoln wrote Stanton. Poor widow Baird's son in the army served a long prison term without much pay. "I do not like this punishment of withholding pay — it falls so very hard upon poor families," Lincoln told the secretary of war. Young Perry from Wisconsin, condemned for sleeping on his post — execution suspended. Charles H. Jonas, prisoner of war at Johnson's Island — paroled for three weeks to go home and see his dying father.

Doggedly Lincoln reviewed the list of Indians condemned to execution in Minnesota, attempting to distinguish degrees of guilt and innocence in individual cases. He ordered Te-he-hdo-ne-cha and thirty-eight others hanged; the army was to protect 300 more in detention from "any unlawful violence." For the larger issue there was no time. "If we get through this war, and I live, *this Indian system shall be reformed,*" he noted.

Friends and other pests were always after the president. "Uncle Jimmy" Short had once saved him from the sheriff in New Salem by purchasing his surveying instruments. Rewarded with a job on a California reservation at $1800 a year, he got fired for gambling with the Indians and cohabiting with a squaw. Not true, complained "Uncle Jimmy." Brother-in-law Clark M. Smith of Springfield on February 7, 1864, asked for a small favor. Smith had accumulated a small fortune in high-priced goods scattered in three stores. Slyly he requested "at a proper time" some notice or a hint that the war was coming to an end, so that he could unload before prices fell. Dr. J. Rutherford Worster certified that his Sandal Sock, made of "wash leather," would preserve the feet on long marches and prevent straggling. Other inventors of devices to hasten victory or ease the suffering of the troops were always at the president, as were sundry ingenious promoters; and duty demanded a review of all. Unable to establish his distance from the war, Lincoln felt its burdens grow steadily heavier.

What damage the enemy could do, Lincoln well knew from the moment of his election. Soon he learned that "to be wounded in the house of one's friends is perhaps the most grievous affliction that can befall a man."

Unity was far from a quality the Union displayed. At first the government and the people did not share an understanding of the country's unprecedented situation. The vague demarcation of powers among the three federal branches created numerous problems, and the political parties were too new and too weak to establish coordination or discipline among or within them.

Lincoln never deviated from his commitment to the rule of law and the constraints of the Constitution. To Chase he explained in September 1863 that he would not take any step simply because he considered it "politically expedient and morally right." To do so would "give up all footing upon constitution or law" and pass into "the boundless field of absolutism," thereby setting back the very cause he sought to advance.

However, Lincoln could not concede that the Supreme Court responsible for *Dred Scott,* on which Taney sat until his death in 1864, was the sole custodian of constitutionality. Like Jefferson and Jackson, the president believed himself as qualified to act in his own sphere in accordance with his understanding of that covenant's meaning as were the judges in theirs.

The legislative branch was more complex, for the Republicans owed their control to the withdrawal of the Southerners. Measures that raised the tariff, that provided for homesteads and land grant colleges, and that established a national banking system, important as they were, enjoyed widespread support and created no problem for the president. But issues that touched on the war, on slavery, and on future reconstruction repeatedly shattered the Congress, leaving recalcitrant fragments not readily shaped into a majority. The upper house divided from the lower, and each, driven by dissension, split into factions that maneuvered in and out of alliances. Lincoln understood that these groupings made no sense in terms of Republicans and Democrats or of radicals and conservatives. Rather he strained to formulate issues that evoked support wherever he might find it, conscious always that his actions were subject to ratification by the will of the people.

At the one extreme were the outright southern sympathizers — antiblack, states' rights, peace-at-any-price men. Some Copperheads actually enlisted in the Confederate forces or surreptitiously lent them aid and comfort; others kept their sympathies within the bounds of the law. The latter shaded over into the camp of peace Democrats, who made no commitment to the South but believed the war not worth fighting and sought a reasonable armistice or compromise, whether it restored the old Union or not. Vallandigham straddled the two positions. McClellan represented Democrats of another sort, who wished to bring the war to an honorable close — one that would restore the Union as it had been and in return offer the South ironbound guarantees of its peculiar institution.

Republican ranks were as brittle. In the halls of Congress, in many a governor's office, and even within the cabinet, the unspoken question hovered over the election of 1864: Why not me? In experience, party following, and polish others believed themselves as qualified as the president, and where ambition led, the perceived call of duty followed. These men and others sincerely criticized Lincoln's policies. He went too fast or too slow, too far or not far enough — in whatever direction was at issue at the moment. Abolitionists believed that he should have freed the slaves immediately, and romantics lulled by visions of the blacks' childlike innocence and wisdom wanted immediate political and social equality. Party hacks wanted somehow to use the conflict to ensure a permanent national Republican majority. Former Whigs sought more restraint, less disruption. Calls for immediate peace negotiations mingled with those for a more vigorous prosecution of the war. Restoration of the South as it had been was the desire of some; total destruction, that of others. Horace Greeley continued to gyrate wildly. In the summer of 1864 he begged Lincoln to yield for the sake of "our bleeding, bankrupt, almost dying" country. Almost alone, Charles Sumner, who often disagreed, understood Lincoln's dilemma: how, in the midst of war, to govern by consent and yet to elicit support for what was right.

The president successfully contained these divisive forces. The state elections in the fall of 1863 tested the extent to which people supported the draft, the Emancipation Proclamation, martial law, black soldiers, and the other war measures. Peace Democrats were out in full force; and Vallandigham in Canada ran in absentia for the governorship of Ohio. Aware of the weariness with war, Lincoln directed his argument mainly to those not for "force nor yet for dissolution" but for some "imaginable compromise." Peace, when it came, would prove once and for all that among free men there could be "no successful appeal from the ballot to the bullet" and that those who took such an appeal were sure to lose their case and pay the cost.

Lincoln's worries that year were unfounded. The electorate gave him a resounding vote of confidence. In Ohio the Union candidate for governor, John Brough, defeated Vallandigham by more than 100,000 votes. "Glory be to God in the highest," Lincoln exclaimed. "Ohio has saved the nation." New Jersey was the only state in which Union candidates lost.

War or no war, the president resolved to conduct an orderly campaign in 1864 and, if necessary, to hand over power in a fashion that would best help the next administration succeed. He was struggling to maintain a government, not to overthrow it. A sense of obligation to the people both on principle and under the Constitution made their will the ultimate law for all. If they deliberately resolved to have immediate peace even at the loss of their country and their liberty, no man had the power or the right to resist them. "It is their own business, and they must do as they please with their own." Lincoln however believed they still wished to preserve "their country and their liberty, and in this, in office or out of it," he resolved to stand by them. In August 1864 he prepared transition plans to hand over power should the election go against him.

For a time in 1863 he was noncommittal about a second

term. No president since Jackson had served more than four years, and the single term had become almost traditional. But early in 1864 he knew that reelection alone would demonstrate that the people approved of his policies of emancipation and reconstruction. A change of administration would be "virtually voting him a failure." He felt himself "not entirely unworthy to be intrusted with the place" he had occupied since 1861. Though perhaps not the very best man for the job in the country, he recalled "a story of an old Dutch farmer who remarked to a companion once that 'it was not best to swap horses when crossing streams.' "

He faced strong Republican opposition. A pamphlet sponsored by his own party blamed him for the war's senseless carnage. "The cant about Honest Old Abe was at first amusing, it then became ridiculous, and now it is absolutely criminal." One correspondent reported that not a single senator favored his reelection. Orville Browning, an old friend who liked Lincoln personally but had long suspected his lack of ability, now sadly noted, "Still, I thought he might get through, as many a boy has got through college, without disgrace, and without knowledge." Alas, Browning concluded, "I fear he is a failure."

The search for an alternative got under way. James Gordon Bennett promoted Grant, and Horace Greeley favored Chase. Grant, loyal to Lincoln, thought his defeat would be a national calamity. But Chase, eager to run, made no secret of his contempt for the president. In February 1864 the Pomeroy Circular, printed in the newspapers, argued that reelection was impossible, that another term would in any case be disastrous because the president was a trimmer guided only by expediency, and that the best man for the job was Chase. Lincoln, unconcerned on the surface, proceeded to chop this rival to pieces. Henry Raymond of the *New York Times,* Lincoln's political manager, wooed Sumner away from the opposition and persuaded Union leagues and local conventions in state after state to announce for the president. Meanwhile in Washington Frank Blair, Lincoln's wily political ally, began to float rumors about the Treasury (of which Chase was secretary), reputedly the most corrupt and profligate department in the capital. The Chase boom collapsed when even the Ohio Republicans abandoned their favorite son. On March 5, 1864, Chase withdrew his candidacy.

Thereupon Governor John A. Andrew of Massachusetts and William Cullen Bryant of New York organized a new movement, with John Charles Frémont their favorite; and their caucus in Cleveland threatened to split the party. But Frémont was like Jim Jett's brother, Lincoln said. "Jim used to say that his brother was the damndest scoundrel that ever lived, but in the infinite mercy of Providence, he was also the damndest fool."

In the end the president used a cabinet reshuffle and patronage to rally the party, and supporters had the convention delegates well in hand. Lincoln did not care who his running mate would be; the post went to Andrew Johnson, a border state man and war Democrat. But the platform had to have a plank calling for a constitutional amendment to outlaw slavery everywhere in the land. All the Republicans fell into line when the Democrats nominated General George B. McClellan, who promised to restore both the Union and slavery. Even Greeley promised to "fight like a savage" for Lincoln, out of hatred for McClellan. That promise did not inhibit the intrepid editor from joining other malcontents in September in an appeal to the president to step down in favor of an (unnamed) stronger candidate. The Democratic *New York World* snickered that it was harder to tell which group hurt Lincoln most, the "manly opponents" who attacked him frontally or the friends who stabbed him in the back.

Although early state polls were close, the election on November 8 gave Lincoln a majority of almost half a million votes, out of some 4 million cast.

Lincoln took the election as a test of whether any government not too strong for the liberties of its people could be strong enough to maintain its own existence in great emergencies. Political divisions did not paralyze people "put to the utmost of their strength by the rebellion." The election demonstrated that a popular government could sustain a national election in the midst of a great civil war. It showed how sound and how strong the United States was.

Planning for reconstruction had no such precise outcome; nor could Lincoln cope with its challenges in ordinary political terms. His view of the constitutional issue was simple. The secession ordinances had never been valid. Therefore the states in the Confederacy had never left the Union. They were in rebellion, and that constituted a military problem with which the president dealt as commander in chief. He could outline the conditions that would satisfy him the rebellion was over, whereupon they would resume their places in the Union. He insisted on no specific plan and would accept whatever met his criteria of restoring constitutional legitimacy. But only his authority was broad enough to establish loyal civilian rule. The War Department, the army, and the executive branch were best appointed to deal with the enormous problems associated with the return of the South to the Union.

By the middle of 1863 the Union army had liberated Tennessee and occupied sections of Arkansas, Louisiana, Texas, Florida, and Virginia. Lincoln then determined to lay the groundwork for a policy that would survive even if he were no longer in office after 1864.

Military regimes in Louisiana, Arkansas, and Tennessee rallied the southern Unionist minority and set up state governments loyal to Washington and committed to liberation. Andrew Johnson, military governor of Tennessee, and Nathaniel P. Banks in Louisiana received instructions to keep enemies out, to organize local administrations, and to draft new state constitutions that ratified the Emancipation Proclamation.

To reconstruct the Louisiana government Lincoln hoped for "a new Constitution recognizing the Emancipation Proclamation and adopting emancipation in those parts of the state to which the proclamation" did not apply. He believed too that while the state was at it "it would not be objectionable to her to adopt some practical system by which the two races could gradually live themselves out of their old relation to each other, and both come out better prepared for the new. Education for young blacks should be included in the plan." Even proslavery people there had strong enough reason to place themselves "again under the shield of the Union, and to thus perpetually hedge against the recurrence of the scenes through which we are now passing."

Sumner and some of his colleagues, however, thought that only Congress had jurisdiction over reconstruction. Motives varied. Some argued that the South, on secession, had reverted to the conditions of territories, subject like others to congressional control. Others feared a compromise that would readmit former states to the Union with slavery intact. Still others suspected the loyalty of Union Southerners. The only loyal Southerners, Sumner said, were the slaves, and citizenship and the right to vote were the only certain guarantees of their freedom. Some Republicans in addition regarded black suffrage as a means of sustaining the party's future control over the region. Of course others violently opposed this course. Former slaves, given the right to vote, would also run for office, and the horrors of "amalgamation, equality and fraternity" would follow.

Lincoln hoped to avoid extremes by making his own moderate approach palatable. To that end a special proclamation, appended to his congressional message, virtually outlawed the old Southern rulers to prevent them from outvoting the loyalists and regaining power. The president refused to pardon, and thus disqualified from voting or holding political office, those who held civilian or diplomatic posts under the Confederacy; those who served as rebel officers above the rank of colonel; those who had resigned from the United States armed forces, Congress, or the judiciary to help the rebellion; and all those who treated captive Union soldiers as bandits or anything other than prisoners of war. Other Confederates would receive a full pardon when they took an oath of allegiance to the United States. Once their number equalled 10 percent of the voters, in 1860, those who had taken the oath could establish a civilian government and elect United States representatives. Their states would then return to the Union with full federal protection. They could not, however, tamper with the Emancipation Proclamation or with laws dealing with the slaves. To abandon the blacks now not only would be to relinquish a lever of power but also would be a cruel and an astounding breach of faith. Temporary control of the freedmen as "a laboring, landless and homeless class" was tolerable as long as the state recognized their permanent liberty and provided for their education.

Lincoln explained that this was only a proposal, and he was prepared to entertain other and better plans. He knew that reconstruction would vary with circumstances, and he solicited congressional cooperation, conceding that either house could refuse to seat representatives from the reconstructed states. The message read to Congress on December 9, 1863, satisfied everyone except hard-line Democrats.

Lincoln tried to implement his 10 percent plan in Louisiana. Loyalists there elected moderate Michael Hahn as governor and chose delegates to a constitutional convention, which outlawed slavery but established a segregated public school system. Lincoln approved of the outcome as the best attainable under the circumstances and proceeded to take similar steps in Arkansas, Tennessee, and Virginia.

Circumstances changed in the spring of 1864 as victory and the presidential election approached. Partisanship and idealism fed the attack on Lincoln. Some congressional Republicans now doubted whether his program would adequately transform the South. Inadequate protection of the former slaves left them open to exploitation by former masters. Reconstruction along Louisiana lines would render the war's slaughter worthless. Negro suffrage was the only answer, Sumner argued. Yet

Lincoln was aware that blacks could not vote in most northern states, and to raise the issue would be disastrous for Republicans in November. But he also recognized the validity of Sumner's fears and suggested to Governor Hahn in Louisiana that only the best educated freedmen receive the right to vote. To make black suffrage a condition of reconstruction would lose the support of white Loyalists, the very people on whom he now called to return to the Union which, imperfect as it was, was the best available for the time being.

Maryland Congressman Henry Winter Davis, who had lashed out at Lincoln's 10 percent plan, and Senator Wade produced a tougher bill that enlarged Congress's role in reconstruction but still lacked a black suffrage provision. The measure prohibited slavery in all the reconstructed states and required a majority of voters to take an "iron clad" oath of allegiance before they could establish a new government. It also excluded all ex-Confederates from participation in the process.

Lincoln vetoed the bill. He denied the authority of Congress to prohibit slavery in the reconstructed areas. The president had done so on the ground of military necessity, using his war powers. Apart from that a Constitutional amendment was necessary. Furthermore Lincoln was unwilling to commit himself to any single plan or to set aside the loyal governments in Louisiana and Arkansas. But he approved other features of the bill and offered executive and military assistance to loyal Southerners who wanted to restore their states to the Union in accordance with it.

At the moment, of course, the military outcome was far from certain, the Democratic candidate for the presidency wished to trade a guarantee of slavery for Union, and many Republicans advocated an armistice under any conditions. As late as February 27, 1865, after the failure of the unofficial peace conference at Hampton Roads, Lincoln still had to deny rumors that he was willing to meet with "the Richmond gentlemen." To a supporter who wanted a quicker end to the war, he explained in September 1864 that he was unprepared to accept a peace that "could not be of much duration." The Union could not spare the 150,000 colored soldiers, seamen, and laborers serving it. With their help he could win. "Throw it away and the Union goes with it." Nor could the administration retain the service of these people "with the express or implied understanding that upon the first convenient occasion, they are to be re-inslaved. It can not be, and it ought not to be."

The Thirteenth Amendment was the appropriate means by which to prevent Congress, the courts, or some later administration from reversing the Emancipation Proclamation, "a King's cure for all the evils." Yet in May 1864 the House had rejected the amendment. After the election the president used patronage and persuasion to bring around recalcitrant congressmen. Favorable action finally came on January 31, 1865, by a margin of three votes. The abolition of slavery, Lincoln believed, was the climax of the drama, "the fitting if not indispensable adjunct to the consummation of the great game we are playing."

Little joy it gave him, for he never for a moment escaped the calculation of human costs, brought to his attention in every day's mail. Nor did the irony of events elude him. Looking out across the Potomac, he once observed, "If the people over the river had behaved themselves, I could not have done what I have."

He did not hide from himself what every American knew, the war's terrible impact on business, on property, and on homes. Unprecedented taxation and an enormous national debt made heavy demands on the population, but not so heavy as consciousness of lives destroyed, bodies shattered, families bereaved. The "heavens are hung in black" he had said a year earlier; and with him, thousands of wives, mothers, children, and spinsters deprived of husbands, sons, fathers, and wedding partners asked, Why? For what?

Only in one way could Abraham Lincoln and his fellow countrymen make sense of the frightful costs of civil conflict.

The purposes of the Almighty were perfect and would prevail though erring mortals failed to perceive them in advance. "Surely," the president wrote in September 1864, "He intends some great good to follow this mighty convulsion which no mortal could make and no mortal could stay." The magnitude of the price measured the magnitude of the value.

Nations like individuals suffered punishment and chastisement in this world, he believed. Americans had prospered but had forgotten God. Intoxicated with success they had become too self-sufficient to feel the necessity of redeeming and preserving grace. Perhaps the awful calamity of civil war, which had desolated the land, was but a punishment inflicted for presumptuous sins, preparatory "to the needful end of our national reformation as a whole People."

The United States was passing through a trial to test whether a government conceived in liberty could endure. Lincoln did not claim to have controlled events, but confessed plainly that events had controlled him. "Now, at the end of three years struggle the nation's condition is not what either party, or any man devised or expected. God alone can claim it." God now willed the removal of a great wrong and willed also that the North as well as the South should pay fairly for complicity in that wrong. "Impartial history will find therein new cause to attest and revere the justness and goodness of God."

No more than earlier did Lincoln presume to define what he meant by God, the Almighty, History, or Necessity — much less identify those terms with the creed, ritual, or mode of worship of any organized body. But he did not waver in the belief that men's "most strenuous efforts would avail nothing in the shadow of His displeasure," would yield no result without "Divine interposition and favor," and would melt in futility without conversion of the nation to awareness of the issues involved.

At first the Union had seemed the issue, made so by secession, which violated the Constitution. Then the issue had become slavery. He himself had always been naturally antislavery, Lincoln told a Kentucky delegation in March 1864. If slavery was not wrong, nothing was. But his oath of office forbade him "to practically indulge" his abstract judgment, until reflection on the possibility of a premature peace persuaded him "that measures, otherwise unconstitutional, might become lawful by becoming indispensable to the preservation of the constitution through the preservation of the nation." The war demonstrated that the house could only survive if it were all free.

Then too, in those trying days and nights, A. Lincoln gave much thought to the meaning of freedom, a hard word to define, for he knew that some men interpreted it as the ability to do what they pleased with others. He was reminded of a shepherd who drove away the wolf from the sheep's throat, for which the sheep thanked him as its liberator. But for the wolf the shepherd was the destroyer of liberty, "especially as the sheep was a black one." Those who appealed to God and humanity to aid them in doing to a whole race what they would let no man do to themselves "contemned and insulted God and His church, far more than did Satan when he tempted the Savior with the Kingdoms of the earth." The devil's attempt was no more false and far less hypocritical.

Having spoken those words, in May 1864, Lincoln added, "But let me forbear, remembering it is also written 'judge not, lest ye be judged.' "

Unable to take refuge in utopianism, pressed by the realities described in his mail, the president agonized over each decision. As peace approached, he dreaded the intemperate passions reconstruction problems would bring into play. To Northerners who wanted a clean sweep in the South, he recalled that Louisiana's constitution, ratified under his 10 percent plan, was "better for the poor black men than [the one] we have in Illinois." He hoped sooner to "have the fowl by hatching the egg than by smashing it." When Sumner protested that "the eggs of crocodiles can produce only crocodiles," Lincoln worked out a suffrage compromise only to have hotheads on both sides shoot it down, leaving the whole question unresolved.

By then too he had discovered the still broader context within which Americans would consider the meaning of liberty. Back in 1863 he had told an Ohio regiment that he occupied "this big White House" but temporarily, a living witness "that any one of your children may look to come here as my father's child has." The struggle of the moment was not simply to free blacks but to sustain a government that guaranteed each "an open field and a fair chance" for industry, enterprise, and intelligence, to assure all of "equal privileges in the race of life, with all its desirable human aspirations." He expressed those thoughts at about the same time that he formulated for Gettysburg the phrases, "of the people, by the people, for the people." Economic and social changes, then in process, would make those assurances far more difficult to deliver than in the Indiana or Illinois of his youth.

Some six weeks before Good Friday of 1865, Lincoln delivered his second inaugural address in ringing, though shrill, tones.

The struggle not yet ended, he said, had been divine punishment for the sin of slavery, a terrible retribution visited upon guilty people everywhere. Neither side had expected the war to last four years, and neither expected it to end slavery. Each looked for an easier triumph, "and a result less fundamental and astounding." Both read the same Bible, prayed to the same God, and invoked His aid against the other. The prayers of both could not be answered; those of neither were answered fully. The Almighty had His own purpose.

Again Lincoln reflected, "It may seem strange that any men should dare ask God's assistance in wringing their bread from the sweat of other men's faces," then again added, "but let us judge not that we be not judged."

And so the finish neared — language Biblical in derivation,

syntax somewhat archaic, sentences simply balanced, one clause
to offset another, pounding the message into every listener's
mind.

> Fondly do we hope —
> Fervently do we pray, —
> That this mighty scourge of war
> May speedily pass away.
>
> [And] yet, if God wills that it continue
> Until all the wealth
> Piled by the bond man's
> Two hundred and fifty years of unrequited toil
> Shall be sunk,
> And until every drop of blood
> Drawn by the lash,
> Shall be paid by another
> Drawn with the sword,
>
> As was said three thousand years ago,
> So still it must be said
> "The judgments of the Lord, are true
> And righteous altogether."

Yet the worst need not occur. The scourge might pass away.
Charity and firmness could stop the holocaust. That he believed, although without illusions about the certainty of success. As he besought his country, "With malice toward none,
with charity for all, with firmness in the right, as God gives
us to see the right, let us strive on to finish the work we are
in, to bind up the nation's wounds, to care for him who shall
have borne the battle, and for his widow and his orphan — to
do all which may achieve and cherish a just and a lasting peace,
among ourselves and with all nations."

For decades the tones echoed in the hearts of his countrymen.

A Note on the Sources

Roy P. Basler, ed., *The Collected Works of Abraham Lincoln* (9 vols., New Brunswick, N.J., 1953–55); and Roy P. Basler, *The Collected Works of Abraham Lincoln — Supplement 1832–1865* (Westport, Conn., 1974) are excellent compilations. All Lincoln quotations come from Basler, where they may be located chronologically. The lines of the Second Inaugural Address have been divided so that they may be read as they sounded. Harry E. Pratt, *Lincoln 1809–1839* (Springfield, Ill., 1941); Harry E. Pratt, *Lincoln 1840–1846* (Springfield, 1939); Benjamin P. Thomas, *Lincoln 1847–1853* (Springfield, 1936); and Paul M. Angle, *Lincoln 1854–1861* (Springfield, 1933) trace day-by-day activities. Jay Monaghan, *Lincoln Bibliography 1830–1939* (2 vols., Springfield, 1943) lists 3958 books and pamphlets; and Richard Booker, ed., *Abraham Lincoln in Periodical Literature 1860–1940* (Chicago, 1940) adds numerous other items.

Browsers in the vast secondary literature must take pains to distinguish fact from fancy. A flood of publications began with the assassination and transformed a controversial wartime president into a martyr. Countless "Abe and me" stories gained wide circulation. Lincoln's law partner, William H. Herndon, embarked on an oral history project, interviewing people who had known Lincoln in the past, maintaining an extensive correspondence, and originating pointless controversies in a series of lectures.

Few respondents were as honest as George Spears, who knew Lincoln in New Salem. "At the time," Spears said when asked to recall Lincoln's early years, "I had no idea of his ever being President; therefore I did not notice his course as I should of." The question of Lincoln's ancestry, the legitimacy of his mother, Nancy Hanks, and of his own birth have needlessly continued to occupy historians ever since. Herndon also produced the Ann Rutledge romance and was responsible for the furor about Lincoln's religiosity or lack of it. Never a friend of Mrs. Lincoln, Herndon drew a scathing portrait of the first lady, attributing to her his partner's political ambitions — life at home with Mary was such hell that her husband preferred to stay away from it. William H. Herndon and Jesse W. Weik, *Herndon's Lincoln, the True Story of a Great Life* (Chicago, 1889) summed it all up and beat into print the account by the president's secretaries, John G. Nicolay and John Hay, *Abraham Lincoln* (10 vols., New York, 1890). There is an excellent analysis of Herndon's contributions to Lincoln historiography in David Donald, *Lincoln's Herndon* (New York, 1948). The romantic view of the martyred president reached its apotheosis in Carl Sandburg, *Abraham Lincoln; the Prairie Years* (2 vols., New York, 1926), the cruelest thing to happen to Lincoln, said Edmund Wilson, after the shots in Ford's Theater.

Albert J. Beveridge, *Abraham Lincoln 1809–1858* (2 vols., Boston, 1928), to which all subsequent writers have been indebted, set the subject on a more scholarly plane. Benjamin P. Thomas, *Abraham Lincoln* (New York, 1952); and Stephen B. Oates, *With Malice Towards None, the Life of Abraham Lincoln* (New York, 1977) are recent summaries.

In the years between the First and Second World Wars, Lincoln's reputation suffered. Edgar Lee Masters's *Lincoln the Man* (New York, 1931), the most vitriolic product of the debunking school, turned Lincoln into a Spoon River caricature. More important, reexamination of the causes of the Civil War in the light of the experience of 1917 led some scholars to conclude that the conflict was needless and that Lincoln was one of a bumbling generation incapable of avoiding it. Although few twentieth-century historians justified the South's peculiar institution, some argued explicitly or implicitly that slavery would have vanished of its own accord if the Republicans, Lincoln included, had but refrained from attacking it. The horrors of war thus did no good and indeed only led into the subsequent horrors of a misguided reconstruction. That attitude permeated the works of James G. Randall: *Constitutional Problems under Lincoln* (New York, 1926); *Civil War and Reconstruction* (Boston, 1937); and *Lincoln the President* (4 vols., New York, 1945–55) — and also Avery O. Craven, *The Coming of the Civil War* (New York, 1942); and *Repressible Conflict* (University, La., 1939); and U. B. Phillips, *Course of the South to Secession* (New York, 1939). Allan Nevins, *Ordeal of the Union* (8 vols., New York, 1947–71) veered in that direction in its early volumes, then took a somewhat different tack in the later ones.

The point of departure of all the works which argued that slavery would eventually have disappeared without war was enunciated by Daniel Webster in 1850 and frequently repeated by Stephen A. Douglas after 1854: Slavery could never spread beyond its natural limits in the area of existing cotton culture of the then Deep South. The twentieth-century concentration of cotton production in Arizona and California exposes the flimsiness of that assurance. Already in 1859 New Mexico had a slave code and planned to strengthen peonage. See Loomis M. Ganaway, *New Mexico and the Sectional Controversy* (Albuquerque, 1944), pp. 69 ff. Lincoln of course denied that slavery had natural limits within which it would gradually stifle. The recent economic literature on the profitability of slavery sustains his point of view.

There is no want of specialized treatments of aspects of Lincoln's life. Books on "the real Lincoln" and the "Lincoln nobody knows" rival those on his image, North and South, on his view of himself and others' views of him, on his literary genius, knowledge of the Bible, "Lost Speech," personal finances, law partners, business associates, friends, and favorite poets. Percy C. Eggleston, *Lincoln in New England* (New York, 1922); Elwyn L. Page, *Abraham Lincoln in New Hampshire* (Boston, 1924); and Andrew A. Freeman, *Abraham Lincoln Goes to New York* (New York, 1960) are only a few of the titles that retrace and reconstruct his travels down to the minutest detail. His "inner life" has been exposed by amateur psychiatrists who have unsuccessfully applied little-understood psychological concepts to a historical figure. Elliot V. Fleckles has even published a *Psychic World of Abraham Lincoln,* dictated by his dead son Willie from the other world (St. Paul, Minn., 1974). Diligent research will further uncover *Lincoln Never Smoked a Cigarette*; and *Abraham Lincoln on the Coming of the Caterpillar Tractor.*

Dozens of works bear the "Lincoln and" title, ranging from William H. Townsend's *Lincoln and His Wife's Home Town* (Indianapolis, 1929); through F. Lauriston Bullard's *Abraham Lincoln and the Widow Bixby* (New Brunswick, N.J., 1946); and Kenneth A. Bernard's *Lincoln and the Music of the Civil War* (Caldwell, Idaho, 1960); to Milton H. Shutes, *Lincoln and the Doctors, A Medical Life of Abraham Lincoln* (New York, 1933).

An enormous and valuable body of scholarly literature treats the man, the setting, and the issues of his times. Louis A. Warren, *Lincoln's Youth, Indiana Years* (New York, 1959); Benjamin P. Thomas, *Lincoln's New Salem* (Springfield, 1939); and William E. Baringer, *Lincoln's Vandalia* (New Brunswick, N.J., 1949) contain information on the early years. Captain Basil Hall and his wife passed through New Orleans at about the time Lincoln did and described what they saw. The most complete account of life in Springfield is Paul M. Angle, *"Here I Have Lived": A History of Lincoln's Springfield* (Chicago, 1971). Donald W. Riddle examines the congressional career in *Congressman Abraham Lincoln* (Urbana, Ill., 1957), while John P. Frank examines *Lincoln as a Lawyer* (Urbana, Ill., 1961).

Paul Simon, *Lincoln's Preparation for Greatness* (Norman, Okla., 1965) deals with the 1840s. Harry V. Jaffa's provocative *Crisis of the House Divided* (New York, 1959) is the thoughtful analysis of a political philosopher, laden with insight although inclined to impart more consistency and coherence to Lincoln's ideas than was there. It should be supplemented with Robert W. Johannsen, *Stephen A. Douglas* (New York, 1973), for a complete portrait of the great debates. Melvin L. Hayes, *Mr. Lincoln Runs for President* (New York, 1960) deals with the campaign for the White House, as does Reinhard H. Luthin's *The First Lincoln Campaign* (Cambridge, 1944), while Eric Foner, *Free Soil, Free Labor, Free Men* (New York, 1970) describes the ideology of the Republican party and Lincoln's place in it. David M. Potter's *Lincoln and His Party in the Secession Crisis* (New Haven, 1942) tries to determine Lincoln's motivations; and the North's reaction is examined by Kenneth M. Stampp in *And the War Came* (Baton Rouge, 1950). Lincoln's Washington is best described in Margaret Leech, *Reveille in Washington, 1860–1865* (New York, 1941).

Treatments of aspects of Lincoln's presidency include: Harry J. Carman and Reinhard H. Luthin, *Lincoln and the Patronage* (New York, 1943); Wood Gray, *The Hidden Civil War, The Story of the Copperheads* (New York, 1942); Robert S. Harper, *Lincoln and the Press* (New York, 1951); Burton J. Hendrick, *Lincoln's War Cabinet* (Boston, 1946); William B. Hesseltine, *Lincoln and the War Governors* (New York, 1948); George F. Milton, *Abraham Lincoln and the Fifth Column* (New York, 1942); T. Harry Williams, *Lincoln and His Generals* (New York, 1952); John S. Wright, *Lincoln and the Politics of Slavery* (Reno, Nev., 1970); William F. Zornow, *Lincoln and the Party Divided* (Norman, Okla., 1954). The conduct of foreign affairs is examined in Jay Monaghan, *Diplomat in Carpet Slippers* (Indianapolis, 1945), which overemphasizes Lincoln's involvement. For contemporary views of Lincoln see Herbert Mitgang, ed., *Abraham Lincoln, A Press Portrait* (Chicago, 1971); and Harry E. Pratt, ed., *Concerning Mr. Lin-*

coln (Springfield, Ill., 1944). Lloyd Lewis, *Myths After Lincoln* (New York, 1929) examines the transformation of Lincoln's image after the assassination, while Benjamin P. Thomas's *Portrait for Posterity* (New Brunswick, N.J., 1947) describes the changing perceptions of Lincoln in the biographies of the late nineteenth and early twentieth centuries. Edmund Wilson, *Patriotic Gore, Studies in the Literature of the American Civil War* (New York, 1962), though occasionally wrong-headed, is charged with perceptive insights.

Numerous biographies and diaries of the period's major political figures supply additional material. Among them are: Edward Bates, *Diary 1859–1866* (ed. Howard K. Beale, Washington, 1933); Maurice G. Baxter, *Orville H. Browning* (Bloomington, Indiana, 1957); Noah Brooks, *Washington in Lincoln's Times* (New York, 1896); Erwin S. Bradley, *Simon Cameron, Lincoln's Secretary of War* (Philadelphia, 1966); Salmon P. Chase, *The Civil War Diaries* (ed. David Donald, New York, 1954); Charles A. Jellison, *Fessenden of Maine* (Syracuse, N.Y., 1962); Ulysses S. Grant, *Personal Memoirs* (2 vols., New York, 1885–86); Bruce Catton, *U.S. Grant* (Boston, 1954); Jeter A. Isely, *Horace Greeley and the Republican Party 1853–1861* (Princeton, N.J., 1947); John Hay, *Diary and Letters* (ed. Tyler Dennett, New York, 1939); Douglas S. Freeman, *R. E. Lee* (4 vols., New York, 1934–35); George B. McClellan, *McClellan's Own Story* (New York, 1887); William S. Myers, *A Study in Personality: General George Brinton McClellan* (New York, 1934); William T. Sherman, *Memoirs* (2 vols., New York, 1886); B. H. Lidell Hart, *Sherman* (New York, 1929); Lloyd Lewis, *Sherman* (New York, 1958); Carl Schurz, *Reminiscences* (3 vols., New York, 1907–08); Glyndon Van Deusen, *William Henry Seward* (New York, 1967); Benjamin P. Thomas and Harold M. Hyman, *Stanton* (New York, 1962); David Donald, *Charles Sumner and the Rights of Man* (New York, 1970); Gideon Welles, *Diary* (ed. Howard K. Beale, 3 vols., New York, 1960).

Index